My HEART,
EVER His

My HEART, EVER His

prayers for women

BARBARA RAINEY

BETHANYHOUSE
a division of Baker Publishing Group
Minneapolis, Minnesota

"I cried through these pages, finding a friend who knows winter and who finds God within her winter. Barbara's vulnerable reach for God is a poetic invitation to my soul . . . to discover Him, right here in this weak frame of mine."

SARA HAGERTY, bestselling author, *Unseen* and *Every Bitter Thing Is Sweet*

"Stunningly candid, Barbara's prayers of lament will resonate in every woman's heart. Precious few know how to struggle and to do so with the wonder of the gospel. Barbara calls forth lament and allows sorrow to rise, but always lands with praise to our Savior and King."

BECKY ALLENDER, cofounder, The Allender Center

"Barbara Rainey's words speak into the heart of every woman who earnestly seeks God. She graciously shares about the seasons of suffering she has endured as a wife, a mother, and a follower of Christ. Barbara reminds us that our unanswered questions keep us reliant on our one real hope, Jesus."

TERESA COELHO, founder, Power of Modesty

"Barbara's beautifully poetic and personal prayers will help readers to bridge the gap between life's confusing, messy realities and the solid truth of God's Word. In her honest conversations with the Lord, we see evidence of the Holy Spirit's work of intercession, comfort, and guidance leading to renewed peace and steadfast trust."

MARIANNE HOUSEHOLDER, leadership development specialist, Athletes in Action

"*My Heart, Ever His* is more than a compilation of heartfelt prayers and accompanying Scriptures. Barbara Rainey inspires the reader that to commune with God is essential in all seasons of life. It is an unquenchable thirst for more with God."

KAREN LORITTS, pastor's wife, author, speaker, Bible teacher

"In these pages I found my head nodding, my heart validated, and my eyes continually turned to the Lord. Barbara's journey through the seasons of life has produced a rich depth, understanding, and sagacity often missing in today's instant-gratification, quick-sound-bites world."

VIVIAN MABUNI, speaker and author, *Open Hands, Willing Heart*

"These prayers are soul care. Discover the grace awakening of being raw-honest with yourself and God. About anything! Barbara's vulnerable confessions hunger for hope. Her ruminations cry out for divine wisdom. Drink deeply from this outpouring, and you will be encouraged to name your own struggles. Our Father welcomes our voice."

JOANNE THOMPSON, author, *Table Life: Savoring the Hospitality of Jesus in Your Home*

"Barbara's beautiful words and authentic prayers stir your soul to draw closer to God. Her prayers touch every part of your life—when life is easy and when life is painful. The truths of her writing sink down deep to encourage and comfort your very soul!"

ANN WILSON, co-host, *FamilyLife Today*

This collection of prayers
is dedicated to my dearest Friend,
the Holy Spirit.

It was His idea to write these prayers,
planted in the soil of my heart.
His illumination inspired the topics,
provided specific words,
gave clarity
and clear guidance.

Thank You
O Spirit of Christ
for Your unending companionship
and nearness.

I address my verses to the *King*.

May You be pleased.

Psalm 45:1

   Throughout, prayer segments that were inspired by specific passages of Scripture are
indicated by blue text. The corresponding references are in the chapter's footnote.

Contents

INTRODUCTION

Why Pray?

WHO HASN'T FELT prayer is futile? Does God hear? Does He care? we wonder.

These universal questions most often arise out of our disappointments or sorrow. Personal loss of any kind reveals our fears about God and ourselves: Is God in control? Does He see me? How am I supposed to live with what's happening in my life right now?

The Psalms pose similar questions. They are earthy, gritty, raw.

> Why, O Lord, do you stand far away?
> Why do you hide yourself in times of trouble?
>
> PSALM 10:1

David and others wrote these prayers, laments, and songs with words that shock us in our present walking-on-eggshells culture. No one knows what to say or not say for fear of offending at work, at school, with neighbors, or with strangers. Then at church there is an atmosphere of niceness, a false everything-is-okay exterior mask we feel compelled to wear to prove God is making good.

But when we are alone . . . when it's just me and God . . . how do I talk to Him?

How do I *not* offend the Creator of the universe? I feel silly sometimes talking to Him, because normal, shallow relational approaches feel ridiculous or embarrassing before the throne of God Almighty.

Suffering has been a very unwelcome part of my life.

Winter came again recently for me. Not like other winters, for God doesn't copy and paste, but works perfectly and individually for what I uniquely need to know and experience of Him. This new season of loss took a completely different shape from previous winters of my life. A different kind of cold settled in; not the sharp, brutal sub-zero kind, but a cloudy, damp, chills-to-the-bone cold. Like a slowly creeping fog that settles and stays, this season of loss was an ill-defined cloud, daily thickening to zero visibility or lifting enough to see hints of sunshine through the mist.

I've learned through the years that God's light shines the brightest in the darkness, so I should have remembered His faithfulness more confidently. I haven't always seen His glow in the middle of the hardest moments of my life, but over time He has revealed hints of Himself in ways He knew I'd recognize, ways that were best for me.

American poet Emily Dickinson wrote, "The Truth must dazzle gradually, / Or every man be blind."[1] My dear heavenly Father knows I can't see His brilliant glory in the daylight all at once, but glints of His dazzling can be seen from valleys and deep wells if I look up. *If I look up.* That is the key. "The deeper the wells the brighter thy stars shine."[2]

Surprising me, God inspired me to write in this season of loss, to put into words the emotions and experiences of my life as a woman as I rode those rough, relentless, pounding waves. I've never been a good journaler, always afraid someone might read my raw revelations and be shocked at my depravity. But in this season I was fully convinced of my wickedness, and I resolved that if God sees all and loves me, what someone else might see is irrelevant. The ink began to flow.

The Psalms were my daily companion every day for months. The words of groaning, complaining, anguish gave voice to my heart and became comfortably familiar to me. The descriptors of emotion felt right, not rash.

These prayers of mine are not happy life-is-great prayers, though like the Psalms, some are praises for what God has taught me. I've realized I am more drawn to the throne of God when life is hard. When the sun is shining and the days are easy, I just move through life enjoying the ride. The wrongness of hard times presses me to Jesus because I know He understands better than anyone else.

But I stepped into prayer writing slowly, cautiously, and carefully. I wasn't sure I could or should be as real as the psalmists.

Adding to my fear of such blunt honesty were memories of my strong teaching to my children to not complain. We memorized as a family, "Do all things without grumbling or disputing" (Philippians 2:14). When my children complained, my comprehension of God expanded as I recognized what He endured from me, from us all, when I grumbled. I'd understood, and I didn't want to be a gripy child of God.

The story of the children of Israel being condemned to wander the desert for forty years because they complained actually frightened me at one point in my life. Paul recounts the story in his first letter to the Corinthians and ends with these words, "[We must not] grumble, as some of them did and were destroyed by the Destroyer. Now these things happened as an example . . . for our instruction" (1 Corinthians 10:10–11). I had vowed not to complain as some of the Israelites had.

Then there is Job. His story also curtailed my prayers. He complained to God repeatedly, voluminously, and God rebuked him. Being a firstborn pleaser, I wanted to please God, make Him proud of me as His daughter. So my prayers for years tended toward nice, monitored, and proper.

But then I saw by my repeated reading in the Psalms that all but one out of one hundred fifty end with words of praise and adoration. I recognized the key to bringing my woes to God was turning the pouring out of my heart in complaint to words of surrender and trust before closing with amen.

Also startling me was the deeper discovery that God wasn't offended by my raw, honest complaints *if* my heart returned to faith. God was gently inviting me to fully express myself to Him as my Father, who loved me and knew what I was feeling anyway. He wasn't afraid or offended by my emotions.

So I invite you to read these cries of a woman's heart as if they are your own. Don't scan these prayers, but read them slowly. Even meditate on them. Underline phrases or portions. Write in the margins. Add your own words. Make these petitions your own.

I hope you will see yourself in various details of my story, though you won't in all of them. Women across the globe have much in common; many of our experiences are universal, the most important being our common need for peace in our relationships, rest in our labors of love, and forgiveness for our many heart sins. Every woman of every age needs what only God can provide. I hope my heart cries will call you to Jesus too.

And remember, when you enter the valley of the shadow, "It's impossible to go through life unscathed. Nor should you want to. By the hurts we accumulate, we measure both our follies and our accomplishments."[3] My folly has been faking it before God for too much of my life. Gratefully, my accomplishment has been, by His hand of boundless grace, a rich, deep, new relationship, born out of loss, that I wouldn't trade for anything.

May you write liberally to your King!

Barbara

THE ROCK, 2019

Daughters of the King

Lord, we come to You as sisters,
as daughters of King Jesus.
It is an honor to be named a daughter of royalty!

You know each one of us intimately,
but to our detriment we know very little of You.
We come before You to learn,
to see more of You.
Teach us, Holy Spirit.

For Your gentle, patient teaching we thank You.

Lord, we know Your plans for us are all uniquely designed,
one of a kind.
Unlike the woman next door,
or my friend I admire.
Unlike all the women who have gone before in ages past.
Unlike those to come in generations future.

For this one-of-a-kind plan and design we thank You.

We also know You well enough to
know our days are numbered;
we do not know what tomorrow may bring.

This knowledge is in Your safekeeping
that we might trust You above our own abilities to control,
as we are so prone to do.

For this keeping of our days we thank You.

Gratefully, Lord, we also know some of
Your eternal majestic character:
You are unchanging, the same yesterday, today, and forever.
You are perfect *Love,* and in You all fear is gone.
You are our Rock, the Stability of our times,
our Peace, our *Comforter.*

For these glimpses of Your majesty,
this knowledge of You that centers and secures
as the ground beneath our feet seems at times to shift,
we thank You.

Open our eyes to see You more clearly,
perhaps as never before.
Open our hearts to fall in love with You in new ways,
perhaps as never before.

Grant us the grace to trust You implicitly and find that
You are always enough.

AMEN.

Hebrews 13:8; 1 John 4:18; Deuteronomy 32:4; Isaiah 33:6; Ephesians 2:14; 2 Corinthians 1:3–4

TWO

Resting in Your Plan for Me

Lord God, Worker of all that is good,

It is easy for me to boldly believe
Your good and sovereign control over all
as I look at the lives of others from afar.

In my friend's life,
when she is struggling, suffering,
wondering what You are doing in her world,
I can so easily say in my heart, if not with my mouth,
"God knows what He's doing.
He will bring good from this."
I mean well.

And it is true.
You alone work all things *together* for good.

Ah, but when it's my life suddenly interrupted
by a medical issue or crisis,
when You bring or allow *calamity*
that affects my world, my people,

when my hopes and dreams are derailed or dashed,
when my prayers are answered only with silence,
then my faith feels fragile.
I feel unmoored . . . adrift . . .
my previous confidence in Your good and sovereign control
leaking rapidly like air from a punctured raft.

Thank You, my Savior,
that You never *change*,
even though my life sometimes jolts and drops
like a roller coaster.

You are my Hiding Place,
my constant Companion, my Comforter,
the *Stability* of my times,
my Security.

Even when my life feels in turmoil from calamity,
You are intimately *acquainted* with my every need,
my every longing.
You are always working in thousands of ways I cannot see
and will never know.

My Father, the great I AM,
Holy Spirit, my Teacher, my Guide, my Helper,
reveal Your truth that I may be free.

Turn my unbelief into belief that all my yesterdays,
every new today,
and each dawning tomorrow will show me
You are enough for me,
and always will be.

I love You, Jesus.

AMEN.

MANY TIMES IT has been true of me that I fall into unbelief, fear, or panic when my life circumstances change. My friend Susan Yates says, "Stability is not the norm, change is." Oh, how we want stability to be our norm!

Several years ago I discovered Isaiah 33:6, "And he will be the stability of your times." As if surrounded by flashing lights, these words shouted to me, "You can always have stability in life if you are looking for it in Me."

And that's the challenge.

I look for security everywhere but in God alone. That's my natural bent. But He wants me to look to Him daily because none of us knows what tomorrow will bring. When I start from that place, looking to Jesus for my stability and security, then I'm less shaken when the unexpected comes.

Romans 8:28; Isaiah 45:6–7; Hebrews 13:8; Isaiah 33:6; Psalm 119; John 14–16

THREE
In Need of Sleep

FINALLY.
I slide into the embrace of sheets,
sigh, exhale deeply.
Eyelids close.
Day is done.

Almost asleep
consciousness floating
dreams alighting.
Breathing.
Deeply.

A cry.
Suddenly alert
Eyes wide
Thoughts flitting
I know baby ate enough.
Is it just a dream? Will she go back to sleep?
Will I?

Unbidden,
I remember an intended task undone.
A promise unfulfilled.

To-do list comes into focus, in the dark.
Guilt settles in
sleep flies.

My beloved's rhythmic sounds of sleep
A child's hand on my arm: "Mommy, I'm afraid."
Familiar regular cramping returns
hot flashes follow
reminding me again . . .
I am woman.

Lord, You, know
when I sit down and when I *rise* up;
You see me here in this bed
needing sleep for the work You have given me.
You know my *path* and my lying down
and are acquainted with all my *ways.*

Lord, You are
the same yesterday, today, and *forever.*
It is I who change.
It is Your constancy I need.

Give me grace
to adjust to these undesired regular sleep interruptions,
to know Your peace because mine is insufficient.

Help me surrender
to these small momentary trials,
because You are with me.
Here. Now.

And
"what if
a thousand sleepless nights
are what it takes to know You're near"?[4]
Satisfy me with Your presence.

Jesus my Shepherd,
lead me, keep me, feed me
give me
R E S T.

A M E N.

INTERRUPTED SLEEP HAS been a companion of mine for
most of my married years. And it is true for most women of all
ages and stages of life.

I have been angry that my husband can sleep through anything, but I learned anger only made falling sleep even more difficult. I've memorized verses to repeat when I'm awake at night.
Though there is great value in memorizing Scripture, repeating

many words never seemed to keep my mind from wandering to other things once my brain neurons were firing. Another tactic I've tried is to sing praise songs to turn my mind away from its tendency to worry and work in those sleepless hours. It is a good discipline, but not a guaranteed off switch for wakefulness.

I have found no solution other than this: Give thanks in all things and talk to God. Redeem the wakeful minutes or hours by talking to Him or even turning on your light and reading His words to you.

Ask God to make the minutes or hours count as you trust Him, waiting for sleep to arrive. All of life is learning to trust and rest in Him as a child.

Knowing God is with me as I lie awake, remembering He sees and knows and understands, is a great comfort and gives me peace.

One day this small struggle will be no more, for He promises us all eternal rest. However, I doubt I will be catching up on sleep in heaven, for "there will be no more night" (Revelation 22:5 NIV); and there will be so much to discover I won't want to sleep!

May you learn with me to rest in His presence, giving thanks in all things.

Psalm 139:2–3; Hebrews 13:8

FOUR

Upon Awaking

My limbs leaden this morning
My head pounding
My thinking dull from interrupted sleep

Jesus, did You ever feel this way?
You were fully human.
You too experienced interrupted sleep.

Paul wrote *in sleeplessness* on his list of hardships,
explaining in everything he trusted You,
and so must I.

In my kitchen
coffee helps but can't dispel the sluggishness.
Multiplied needs of others
assail me;
my calendar's commitments . . . must be kept . . .
but seem too much . . .
How will I press through?

"I am *sufficient,*" You said.
"My power is perfected in *weakness.*"

I believe this is true,
but will You be enough for me today?

A bolt of supernatural energy
lifting my lethargy
would sure be nice, Lord.
But that kind of power from on high
has never been given to me.

Interrupted sleep has been mine
repeatedly
over and over and over
for decades of seasons.

Newborn needs and toddler demands
middle-schooler and teen dramas
college kids' wanderings and dangers
empty-nest fears and aging aches.
Sleep interruptions never cease.

Walk by *faith* and not by sight,
I remember.
For the eyes of the Lord see the *heart*.
He looks for those who are fully His.

Lord, what do You see in my heart?

I see discouragement that I cannot rise above.
I see limited accomplishment ahead,
and the need for a nap.

I wish I were unaffected by my body's rhythms
I wish for vitality
I wish for power to rise above
I wish I weren't so human.

I am wishing for heaven.

I condemn myself when I become impatient,
disbelieving, angry.
But You don't,
for there is *no condemnation* in Christ Jesus.
You love me just as I am
in all my weaknesses and frailties.

O Lover of my soul, You know my frame;
You remember that I am *dust*.
As a father shows compassion to his children,
so the Lord shows *compassion*
to those who fear Him.

Interruptions, infirmities, inadequacies
are mercies in disguise;
treasures of grace wait to be discovered in the darkness,

in the fog of my fatigue,
if I will but ask.

Here I am, Lord,
needing sleep.
Help me.
I will trust You, believe You are with me,
believe You are enough
for my needs.

AMEN.

WHEN I IMAGINE Jesus living with morning fatigue, interrupted sleep, and the continual press of people needing, wanting His attention—as I'm sure was very true about His life—it helps me know I am not alone.

Jesus loved the women around Him. He had compassion on their struggles. He has compassion on mine.

And He prays for me before the Father. My devoted Friend and Brother knows my frailties and loves me still. Knowing this is true eases the distress of my soul.

Does such knowledge do the same for you?

May you run to Him in your need. He will never turn you away.

2 Corinthians 6:5 NASB; 12:9; 5:7; 1 Samuel 16:7; Romans 8:1; Psalm 103:13–14

FIVE

Husbands

My husband
so completely other than me.
Not just opposite.
Foreign.

How could anyone think male and
female are interchangeable?
Are You sure Eve came from Adam, God?

He hears me say I had a rough day.
He says he's sorry, means it,
but he doesn't really know, can't feel what I feel.
His chemistry, DNA, every molecule
so unlike mine.

Many are our differences for good:
he is stronger, more objective,
willingly will defend me
and our kids
from foes real and invisible.

Even though he is a great gift to me
in countless ways,
it is still easy for me to become critical.

Even after decades
of faithful love, demonstrated sacrifice,
I can feel at times unknown, unloved, uncared for.

I know I'm not always easy to love.
I change
more than I would like
and I don't always know why.

One day his teasing is funny,
another day it hits me wrong,
and he's confused, bless him.

One day my helpfulness is helpful,
he is appreciative.
Another day my helpfulness is perceived as controlling;
tension bristles.

Some days we are like coarse sandpaper
scratching as we pass.
I grumble quietly at his shoes and socks
still lying on the living room floor,

or bruise with snippy words
about his favorite tees, his habits, his patterns.

Other times we live our days in harmony
like choreographed rowers
gliding across hidden currents, secret depths
with beauty, ease, and grace,
completely forgetting past days of disunity.

I cannot imagine how those who don't know You
manage male and female disparity,
relational rifts,
vast differences that clash
or constantly constrain.

It is Your Spirit
who makes my half of this relationship
sail or smolder.

Only You can make
two impossibly different
jigsaw pieces fit together
to create a marvel of beauty.

Oneness Maker,
remind me to give *thanks* every day
in all things

for all differences even though they sometimes grate.
Giving thanks releases me to freedom,
honors Your choosing of us,
welcomes Your Spirit's work.

Once again,
I surrender my heart to You,
knowing my bankrupt soul
cannot do this union work alone.
Help me, my Savior.

AMEN.

1 Thessalonians 5:18

SIX

Answers Unseen

I prayed for strength for today.
Did You hear my request, Lord?
Do You see my need?
I don't feel stronger, more vibrant,
more alive.

Does that mean You didn't answer?
Or is Your strength invisible,
a kind I can't feel?
Are You working in me in ways I can't see or touch or feel?

Endurance, You say,
grows in the hard soil of testing.
Do the trials of my faith
sow unseen seeds within?

Is my soul a vast farm,
an estate with plots of soil tilled for fruit
and produce I can't imagine, can't see
that You want to plant and grow?

Protein drinks, nutrition bars, super foods
seem an easier solution to my fatigue dilemma.

All promise endurance, noticeable, measureable,
life-changing.
But the kind You have in mind,
I think,
is not the same.

Do not lose heart, You remind me.
Though my outer visible body is *decaying*,
not performing for me as I desire and wish,
my heart, my soul is being changed
day by day.

My inner life is being *renewed* invisibly.
You alone see our hidden work there,
long, bare furrows, broken, carved
open by Your tilling hand,
ready for Your planting.
Our cooperative partnership,
Your Spirit nudges mine: "I'm sowing. Trust Me."
My quiet choice, "Yes, Lord,"
is unseen.

But perhaps not.
Maybe You are measuring my growth
as we parents measure our children's growing stature.

Are You recording my baby faith steps
in one of Your many books?
Nothing is hidden from Your sight.

Though I don't feel renewed strength,
I do feel comforted by knowing
You are pleased, Abba Father, that I come to You.

Lord, help me rest, relax,
knowing You always hear my every prayer.
And help me trust You with Your secret soul work,
to remember the things which are unseen
are *eternal.*

AMEN.

James 1; 2 Corinthians 4:16, 18

SEVEN

This Present Detour

I plan.
Always thinking ahead
making to-do lists
anticipating events, birthdays, meetings,
calendar ever in view.

Worthy are my goals,
I believe,
for good, for others, for the kingdom.

No time allotted on my calendar for
carousing, impurity, *dissensions*, cunning, or evil;
certainly this pleases God.

So why, Lord,
interrupt my work for You?
Stopped by the flu,
set aside by bronchitis, slowed by a nameless virus,
this present detour labeled
chronic hives.

Hours for writing,
creating, studying,

now consumed by research on diets
deciphering unreadable words on labels
adding uticaria, doxepin, Xolair to my vocabulary
achieving frequent-flier status
at the pharmacy.

My sweet friend is living with severe headaches,
another with MS.
"In this world you will have *trouble*,"
said the Master.
I'm always surprised by trouble,
as if He spoke falsely.

How long, *O Lord*,
how long?
I plead after eight long weeks
of daily dozens of large itching welts.

Your many prophets, David, and the psalmists
cried these word before You too.
They wondered as do I,
Does God see?
Does He care?
What is He doing with me?
Will God heal?
Or will this be my new normal?

This present detour befuddling
brings discouragement.
Jesus knows.
He understands.
That His life may be *manifested* in my body,
in my mortal flesh.
That my frailty,
my cracked pot might reveal the treasures of His light.

Hope of all things working for *good*,
faith in His *promise* to never leave or forsake
become very real in this detour.
Sufferings prepare me for eternity.
I comprehend that more clearly now.

His unchanging love . . .
undeterred by my present condition or productivity.
He loves me, wants my attention.
And now He has it.

Teach me, Lord, in these days no matter how long they last.
May I hear You, see You,
love You more than ever.

AMEN.

_____

Galatians 5:19–21; John 16:33; Psalm 13:1; 2 Corinthians 4:11; Romans 8:28; Hebrews 13:5

EIGHT

Unseen

Jesus,
You spent thirty years
waiting
in obscurity,
hidden
unseen
unknown.

Mothers understand.
We too live in obscurity,
working, teaching, correcting, praying,
hidden
unseen
unknown
at home.

Only one snapshot remains
in the photo album of Jesus' childhood.
Mary, frantic, worried about her son
left behind,
oblivious to the multitude dangers she imagined.

Moms identify,
our children, even those grown,
unaware of dangers we imagine,
fears we see.
Help us to trust You as we wait
on a future only You see.

Jesus, my Savior,
in Your unseen years,
Did You see needs You knew You could meet,
diseases You could have healed,
children dying You could have resurrected?

More lives could have been changed,
more good done,
had unseen obscurity not been Your lot.
You could have been known!

I see projects I want to tackle
people I need to meet
places I want to explore
talents I want to develop
a ministry I want to start.
But my children . . .
their unending needs shackle me

restrain me
from all I could be.

How could waiting
to write
to speak
to paint
to start a business
be wise
when there is so little time?

It is incomprehensible
mysterious
baffling
to us,
Jesus' perfect trust of the Father
to wait patiently,
to endure years of days
unseen
hidden
unknown
until the *fullness* of time had come.

My waiting
such a personal inconvenience.

His, an accepted essential part of the perfect plan.
Content to wait,
To listen for His Father's voice
for the acceptable time,
the perfect time.

O my Father,
whose time is always perfect and precise,
help me wait, trust, listen
as Jesus did.
Save me from rushing ahead.

And if I'm never known
seen
recognized
beyond my family and my little world,
let me be content
knowing You see.

You are my audience
of One.

No one else matters
but You, my Jesus!

AMEN.

I'VE TALKED TO many young moms who feel guilty that they don't have a blog or write books or lead a ministry or run a business. I understand the pressure in this generation, when so many young women are achieving fame and renown in their thirties and early forties with books and ministries established in their names.

It's too easy with social media to compare. And it's hard to believe your work at home matters, when it seems all you hear are complaints instead of compliments from your kids.

Recently, I had another one of these conversations with a young mom. I was sharing with a small group my conviction that there is a cost to be paid when moms seek to "do it all." Someone in the family will suffer from her lack of presence, I said. A child's needs can't be predicted and therefore scheduled. Moms (and dads too) have to be present when the needs are expressed.

Being present from baby years to teen years is invaluable for the stability and emotional health of your children. Building the life, soul, emotional maturity, and faith of your children cannot be delegated.

Mothering is such an important ministry. There are only a few years to build into children, only a very few years to be the most important person in their lives. God made them to need us, to draw their life from us, to find their well-being and security from their one and only mom and dad.

My challenge is to trust God's timing in your life. God's calendar for Jesus' ministry began at thirty. Do we think those ten years of his twenties were wasted? If your life is His, if you belong to God, He owns your present and your future. He wastes nothing.

These years of obscurity, of being unseen, are not without value. Though you aren't often praised in the dailiness of mothering, God sees, and He will reward your diligence.

Galatians 4:4

NINE

Upside-Down Kingdom

Perplexed,
confused, uncomprehending
am I
about You, the Riddle Maker.

I read in Your book
words that baffle me, make no sense:
The *first* shall be last.
Bless those who persecute you.
Consider it *joy* when you encounter trials.

Head-shaking,
this dissonance,
this clash of infinite with finite,
Your transcendence,
my vapor of a life.

The map from my tiny town
to Your kingdom,
not always straight or forward,
Your directions
lettered with mysteries,

layered with parables,
like following clues, not highways.

Your words
contradict my ways.
Beware being noticed by others . . .
Lay up *treasures* in heaven.
Yet punctuated with promises,
Seek first His kingdom and His *righteousness*
and all these things will be added to you,
I hear the King's voice in these words . . .
calling . . . me.

I am a lamb
following my Shepherd Prince
whose rule does not forcefully subjugate
but calls with a still soft voice
whispers my name
tells me I am His own.

This upside-down kingdom,
its law is love . . .
its King, patiently waiting
for more to say yes to His invitation,
more transformed sinners

to be clothed in white
made ready for the marriage feast
of the Lamb.

For decades I have followed
Your counterintuitive lead
as if on a highway from point A to B,
assuming arrivals
mile markers
will note my progress.

But now I'm seeing more clearly,
being made into Your likeness,
not accomplishments,
is always Your goal
as I journey this pilgrim path
to a city whose *architect* and builder is God.

Your paradoxical kingdom is
not of this world.
It is high and lifted up.
Your ways *higher* than my ways.

Until that day
when Your kingdom comes,

You ask me to be low,
as a child,
to see my helplessness
and become happily dependent
because You alone have the *words* of eternal life.

May thy will be done
on earth and in me.

Amen.

Matthew 20:16; Romans 12:14; James 1:2; Matthew 6:1, 20, 33; Hebrews 11:10 NASB; Isaiah 55:9; John 6:68

TEN

The Gamble of God

What an amazing risk
making man and woman in Your image
like You
to represent You,
ambassadors . . .
to carry Your presence
from room to room
place to place
day after day
year after year.

We house this *Treasure*
inside our multihued bodies of earth.
Terra,
shaped,
molded by the fingers of God,
Eden's virgin clay
containers of Your glory.

What is this Treasure?
A sea chest full of gold and jewels?
The value of Greek and Roman

antiquities?
These are but dust.

Let there be *light*
has entered . . . illumined hearts!
His splendor, excellence, majesty
condescended, bent low.
His glory compressed,
hidden in my compromised heart,
my fragile, common clay cracked pot.

Bestowing on us a free will to choose You
not just once and for all
a thousand times we can choose to reject You
and Your way,
go off on our own.

Why this great risk?
You . . . the great I AM,
Ruler, Creator of all . . .
before whom all will one day bow,
Why did You give frail clay pots this freedom?

Of course!
You want to be chosen,
loved freely!

Forced affection is not genuine,
means nothing.

We understand.
Our hearts ache to be chosen
to belong
to be called
to be united with Love.

And so You have done,
You who are Love,
You have chosen me before the foundation of the world,
chosen all
who call upon Your name.

Your presence is to me my greatest Treasure.
You are my *pearl* of great price.
To be Yours
a profound mercy,
a grace beyond comprehension.

Thank You, Jesus,
for choosing me.

AMEN.

2 Corinthians 4:7; Genesis 1:3; Matthew 13:45–46

ELEVEN
Marriage

Why, God, did You create marriage?
my daughter asked,
and sometimes I wonder too.
We all bought happily ever after
and too often it is not.

Your idea was conceived
before Adam and Eve.
Three in One imagined,
a plan to show Your oneness.
Two freewill creatures, formed by You,
together, You declared,
display *Us* to the earth.

This journey has been harder than I ever imagined
on that happy "I do" day.
There were times, Lord, You remember,
when I questioned Your design,
wondered how we'd ever get past the present crisis.

By not quitting we always arrived
on the other side,

with new unseen strengths, endurance built into us,
knowing more love, appreciation, respect
than before,
our foundation anchored more securely,
our relationship better than ever.

You knew marriage would be hard,
Your elegant art
lacerated by many who reject Your plan.
You knew many would not survive,
unbelief and selfish desires would cut short
Your beautifying soul work.
But You knew the risk was worth the glory.

When marriage is lost
not just the institution is harmed,
but wedded participants suffer damage, become cynical,
can no longer pray, hope, believe,
can no longer love purely.
"Disunity destroys both beauty and happiness."[5]

Like an earthquake shaking the Louvre
every divorce, the wrecking of a masterpiece in process;
every marriage ended
spreads unease through the land.

You have planted marriages in every culture
so Your image and love can be seen
in unions of beauty for generations.

We have learned
marriage is to be a beautiful reflection of You
that the power may be of God
not of ourselves.
I'm grateful, Lord,
for this understanding.

Marriage Savior,
no matter what trials lie yet ahead,
I want to be found believing You and Your every word.
I want my marriage to be a beacon,
a light calling others to join us
till death do us part.

May all those who see our committed union
be encouraged with great hope
to believe in You,
because nothing is *impossible* for You.
Even marriage.

AMEN.

Genesis 1:26; Luke 1:37

TWELVE

I'm Afraid

A text
from my child.

"Something is wrong, Mom."

Breath catches, heart stops.
I'm terrified.
Thumbs text questions
mind races
imagining, conjuring, fearing
the worst in the unknown.

My life, her life, will we be okay?
Will what we know today be no more?
Will another loss be mine, ours to bear?

When my child is late coming home
I fear.
Has he been in a wreck?
It was true of my friend.
Her daughter died.

My daughter fears for her unborn babe

knows too many friends who have suffered
miscarriages, trisomy, death
just days after birth.
I fear with her.

Dark thoughts stalk
hands shake
faith stutters
my security in today, stolen.

Taking every thought *captive*
is like herding flocks of birds
wildly fluttering in my mind.
Yet He who created the birds of the air
could with a word tame them.
Why not my fears?

"When my mind acts without thee
it spins nothing but deceit and delusion."[6]
It is true.
You know what tomorrow will bring.

I talk to myself, as I wait for more news.
Even if I walk through the valley of the shadow of *death*
I will fear no evil
for *You* are with me.

I repeat over and over,
You are with me
You are with me
You are sufficient
You are enough
You are with me.

I have been here before, I remind myself.
The way ahead obscured
thick fog heavy all around
eyes, feet, heart unmoored, unsure
I can't go on, I've said times without number.

Every time,
You never left me nor abandoned.
You have always brought me to the other side.
I know You will strengthen and guide again
even if I feel lost,
can't see evidence of Your presence
with me today.

In this moment I choose.
When I am afraid I will *trust* in You.
I will.
Over and over

I will choose,
I will believe.

My Father, my Jesus, my Comforter,
Thank You for this present darkness
by faith.
You are not surprised, caught off guard as am I.

Your plans will not be thwarted.
Your presence with me is unchanged.
You always act in good
and You promise to work all for *good*.

Calm my anxious frightened heart.
And when I again let what-if fears fly,
guide me to surrender them
and my heart to You
Again and again.

AMEN.

DURING THIS SEASON of loss, our youngest announced
her first pregnancy. She loaded apps on her phone for tracking
each day's changes in her growing little one and kept me updated
regularly by text. One day as I was about to board a flight, her

text arrived embedded with fear. As I took my seat on the plane, knowing I would hear nothing for the next two hours, I wrote this prayer not just expressing the fear of the present moment but remembering the multiplied fears of my years as mommy to my six.

David wrote, "For God alone my soul waits in silence. . . . I shall not be *greatly* shaken" (Psalm 62:1–2, emphasis added). I'm so encouraged that strong, brave, powerful King David wrote these words. Feeling fear is not wrong. It is a result of our fallenness. Adam and Eve walked with God daily in the garden of Eden in perfect peace, but the fall ushered in fear. When asked why he crouched in hiding among the trees, Adam explained to God, "I heard the sound of you in the garden, and I was afraid" (Genesis 3:10).

Fear is a constant companion as we walk through this life. But overwhelmingly woven throughout the Psalms is the promise of His presence that calms, protects, and saves us. Though David was shaken, he wrote he would not be *greatly* shaken. There is a difference.

Even when facing our greatest enemy, death, we who believe in Christ can know it is not the end. Death will come, but it will not win. I have felt like my life would fall apart, my body would never recover, my world would never be the same, but in those moments God was with me as He promised. I called upon Him, depended on Him, waited on Him in silence to do His invisible eternal work.

Two hours later, when my plane landed, a text was waiting: "Went to the doctor. All is well." Today my daughter and her husband are in love with a beautiful little boy named Lincoln. We are all grateful God's plan was to give them a healthy baby. We do not take that for granted anymore.

May you be comforted, now or in future times of fear, for as David also wrote, "You are with me" (Psalm 23:4). If you are in Christ, He will never leave you, no matter how shaken you may be.

---

2 Corinthians 10:5; Psalm 23:4; 56:3; Romans 8:28

THIRTEEN

The Comparison Delusion

It started with her eyes.

Something beautiful,
delicious looking,
desirable
beckoned.

Like hers
my eyes are easily distracted,
attracted to other lovelies . . .
imagined relationships,
longings to be like her or her,
secretly glad I'm not like her.

Saying these words to you, my Lord,
makes me feel ashamed
to admit I devalue others this way.
But You already know . . . see . . .
are ready to forgive
and restore my heart from this comparison sin.

My Creator,
my Abba Father,

You made no mistakes
in your creation, fashioning of me.
Your plans are perfect,
always for my good.

Weaknesses, flaws, inadequacies within
that I disdain
are given by You that I might trust You.

Your sufficient grace cannot be known
apart from experiencing need;
perplexities, diseases, failures, imperfections
force me to fall before
Your throne.

And it is very good.

Contentment
with what You have given
is not natural.

Forgive my constantly wandering eyes
comparing, measuring, evaluating
myself against others
instead of fixing my eyes on Jesus,
Author and *Perfector* of my faith.

Your kind providence has established the frame
of my life
and You wisely administer
all that enters my space.

Impress me deeply with a sense
of Your goodness to me in all things,
for You are always
ENOUGH.

AMEN.

Hebrews 12:2

FOURTEEN

To Be Named

A name.

Tree, giraffe, atom, car;
a word carrying
shared knowledge about nature, creatures,
elements of creation, man's inventions.
Vocabularies of common understanding
across nations, tongues, cultures.

In the heavens
billions of nighttime jewels
are known
numbered
named
by the Word.

In the beginning
the Word spoke,
His voice sounded authority,
brought forth life and named,
created language,
gave us words.

We are made like Him
"in Our image
in Our *likeness*," He said,
named male and female by God,
named Adam,
who named Eve.

Everything He created
shall be *called*.
We too,
made in His image to create,
shall call,
bestow names.

To name is power.

Every newborn named by those who, with God, made him.
A painting is named by the artist,
a book by the author,
music by the composer,
newly discovered sea creatures by the marine biologist.

His name is power.

And He shall be called
Wonderful, Counselor, Mighty God,
Everlasting Father, Prince of Peace,

Emmanuel, Bright Morning Star,
Son of David,
Alpha and Omega.

To name bestows meaning,
summarizes knowledge,
declares the named one known.

Love lavishes
nicknames, true names,
set-apart secret names,
family names, honored titles,
each a beautiful facet of our unique identity.

To lose one's name
is to become unknown
void of identity, meaning.

Evil destroys,
wars to make our names perish from the earth,
to kill by calling us
worthless, unwanted, unloved,
to dirty the divine nature within
to make us like Nebuchadnezzar,
who made a name for himself,
then was banished to eat like an ox.

Our Brother knows how this feels.
Jesus, were You bullied, called hurtful names?
"Weak one" because You wouldn't fight back,
"Mom's favorite" because You always obeyed?

Your name carried no prestige or titles,
it was mocked, spoken with derision,
Your earthly home a no-name forgettable place
from which *nothing* good had ever come.

You understand
hurtful names flung, so hard to shake.

From the cross
Your voice calls and
You rename me:
purchased, redeemed, pardoned,
a saint, a royal *priest*, a child of God,
beloved, treasured,
my name inscribed on Your hand,
written in Your *book*!

One day
to those who overcome
a new *name* will be given
written on a white stone

known only by God
and the one to whom it is *given*.
It will be our secret alone, my dear Father.
This knowledge makes my heart sing!

Name above all names,
How *majestic* is Your name in all the earth.
I give thanks to Your *holy name*.
You, O God,
are my everything,
my all in all.

AMEN.

Psalm 147:4; Genesis 1:26; 2:19–20; John 1:46; 1 Peter 2:9; Revelation 21:27; 2:17; Psalm 8:1; 97:12

FIFTEEN

My Heart, His Home

Thank You, Lord,
for my hidden half-pound ticker
which mysteriously yet faithfully has kept me alive
for decades,
its expiration date gratefully not yet met.

The name, heart, a title
for an organ complex and intricate,
but there is another kind.

Jesus, You know all about my physical heart,
my spiritual eternal one too,
for the heart of man is *deep*,
replete with mystery,
meaning beyond my comprehension.

At birth, my heart was made like Yours.
Your Word tells me Yours is pleased,
happy, glad, and laughs;
feels anger, regret, longing, hurt, sadness, and loss.
Love and compassion also Yours.
That I am like my Creator is a wonder.

My heart is a residence too,
a *temple,*
You have said,
through whose windows can be seen what I've stored there.

Like castles of old with secret staircases,
false bookcases, hidden rooms
I used to believe I could find places to hide from You,
unseen cellars for burying certain
feelings, thoughts, desires;
out of the *heart* come evil thoughts,
murder, adultery, immorality,
theft, false witness, slander.
My old heart produced these.

But when You gave me a new heart,
walked through the door my faith opened,
took up residence in my dwelling place,
remodeling . . . restoration began.

You didn't just want to clean out the *secrets* of the heart
and buttress my poorly constructed self-security system,
You also wanted grand new additions.

So You added on a treasury
and began filling it with stories of Your love

memories of Your protections and deliverances
snapshots of Your provisions and goodness.

You constructed a large insulated control room
where Your throne resides.
I meet You there more and more often.
I talk, You listen, I listen to You speak.
And there You offer to rule my flashing, firing
unruly thoughts, emotions, desires, fears
in my fearfully, wonderfully made-by-You dwelling.

You built a library which has slowly filled with tomes
of Your Word,
stored there that I might not sin against You.

And beautiful rooms filled with riches
of Your undeserved grace.
Chambers of my heart named:
noble, persevering, pure, true, gentle.
You have *adorned* me in the hidden person of the heart
with imperishable *beauty*.

Years of Your work
have made my heart not just a castle but a kingdom
with highways to *Zion*
and soil sown with light for righteousness.

Your transforming love transforms mine
then You speed it on to family, friends, strangers.

"Under Construction"
the sign will read till You take me home.
Like flooding rains and winter snows,
waves of doubt and freezing fears
damage this castle, Your dwelling place,
my unbelief hinders Your work,
makes spring repairs necessary . . . repeatedly.

But time has taught me
how liberating Your blueprints for me
how good all the structures You have rebuilt.
More than ever I trust You with my life, my heart.

O Lord, my Master and Builder,
may my heart be *blameless*
wholly devoted and courageous;
may my heart stand in awe of Your words.
And may I never be afraid of bad news,
because my heart is firm, *trusting* in You,
the Lord my God.

AMEN.

Psalm 64:6; Matthew 15:19; 1 Corinthians 3:16; Psalm 44:21; 119:11; 1 Peter 3:4; Psalm 84:5; 97:11; 119:80, 161; 112:7

SIXTEEN

My Dearest Friend

Holy Spirit,
Author of all Grace and Comfort,
we think You silent
if we think of You at all,
forgotten God.

You were sent,
a Gift
to me
to be with me forever
to never leave me or forsake me.
I am not an *orphan*!

You are my Helper,
my Teacher,
my Guide.
In my daily forgetfulness
You help me remember
all that *Jesus* spoke to me
in His Word.

My constant Companion,
my Promise,
my Purifier,
my Power,
You keep me secure,
refine me as silver
strengthen my faltering faith.

And even more,
beyond belief,
Holy Spirit,
You *pray* for me before the Father!
And not me only,
millions of believers worldwide
simultaneously
also indwelt by You.

Are You divided into millions of pieces
and yet not diminished?

Finite inhabited by the infinite,
inconceivable!

Holy Spirit,
Restrainer of evil
hovering this spinning orb,

we have no idea Your preserving power,
how much farther evil would reach
without Your staying hand.

Thank You, Spirit of God,
for these multiplied ways
You save me
and bind me to Jesus.

Gentle powerful One,
Whisperer of *truth* to my heart,
I'm in awe that You condescend to live
within my fractured being.

Breath of life
my very oxygen
strengthen and guide me
today and always.

I worship You,
my dearest Friend and closest Companion.

AMEN.

John 14:18, 26; Romans 8:26; 2 Thessalonians 2:6–7; John 16:13

SEVENTEEN
Marveled

I know amazement,
watched my children's discoveries in this beautiful world,
saw through their fresh new eyes
wonders long forgotten.

Their mistakes, sin, stubborn hearts, outright rebellion
often left me wondering too;
why would they try that . . .
go their own way?
I marveled at the strength of sin,
the weakness of the flesh.

But there is more.
Multitudes of creations by Your imitating creatures:
bridges, buildings, books,
art, dance, music,
jaw-dropping marvels fill us with wonder.
And it is good.

All Your creation inspires awe
from distant galaxies to microscopic miracles
impossible complexity, stunning beauty

intricately impossible designs
call forth amazement and worship.
This too is good.

When You walked the land, Jesus,
Your disciples, hundreds of followers,
even groupies, the skeptical and Pharisees
marveled at Your teaching
for You spoke with authority.

But only twice is it recorded that You, Jesus, marveled.

A centurion,
a Roman foreigner trained in war,
peacekeeping, leadership,
a man with authority over many,
attended by many,
supposedly hard-hearted, cruel, demanding.
But surprised all, cared about his servant,
went to Jesus, asked for His help.

Jesus agreed.
The centurion replied,
"I am not *worthy* to have you come under my roof,
just say the word and my *servant* will be healed."
And Jesus marveled.

"No one in *Israel* has such faith," He declared.

The chosen people of God
out-faithed by their archenemy, a Roman.

In His hometown teaching one Sabbath,
listeners were astonished by His words,
but were offended because He was "just" the son of Mary
with ordinary brothers and sisters.
He could do no *mighty* work there . . .
And He marveled at their unbelief.

The chosen people of God
un-faithed by skepticism, cynicism, deep doubts.

In response
I ask myself,
Jesus, have I been offended by You
as Your neighbors were?
Have I steadfastly clung to my evaluations,
my conclusions about You,
assumed You could do nothing about my troubles,
my sickness, my broken relationships?

Am I so familiar with You and Your story
that I glaze over and dismiss
as did those who'd watched You grow up?

Am I just a listener on the Sabbath
or am I a hearer
who recognizes who You really are,
eager to believe,
willing to risk faith
like the centurion?

My Jesus,
I am a foreigner too, not of Your kin,
but as a Christian sometimes too familiar
have *lost* my first love
don't marvel at Your teaching anymore.
Forgive me.

More than anything, Lord,
I want You to marvel at my faith.
I cringe at the thought of You marveling at my unbelief.

Help me to honor You, love You
and determinedly cling to You
by believing against all odds,
even before I feel,
for
faith is not a feeling.

Make me like the centurion.

May my faith remain steadfast, believing,
abounding in hope,
that I may please You and hear,
"Well done, my daughter."

AMEN.

Matthew 8:8, 10; Mark 6:5–6; Revelation 2:4; Romans 15:13

EIGHTEEN

Soul Sufferings Are His

Accused.
Words spoken.
Suggesting my motives were to steal.
Heart quivered
soul shook.

Another day, another integrity stab
implying my heart's desire for women
somehow inferior
less valuable than men's lofty work.
A joke made,
two men chuckled, oblivious,
my heart wounded.

My husband,
his history of good
minimized
set aside
ignored.
He and I one
I hurt for him.

You know our world, Lord,
full of accusations
from friend and foe,
from self-accusing self,
from our enemy, Satan.
I freely acknowledge I am not perfect,
a transgressor, saved by grace.
Help me trust You with my soul sufferings,
my Redeemer, Restorer, Rescuer.

But it is not I alone who hurt in this broken world.

My friend whose daughter has been missing for two years,
her remains found . . . this week
a funeral planned
a murder investigation begun.
I hurt for her.
How has she coped?

Next day's news . . . another school shooting.
The anguish touches me,
multiplies wounds
theirs, my friend's, mine,
it . . . is . . . too . . . much.

But You, Jesus,
carried *all* our *sorrows*,
bore *all* our griefs;
the *iniquity* of us ALL
fell on You.

My own sorrows small,
sufferings momentary,
yet today feel unbearable.

How did You, Jesus, carry the weight of *all* sin and *all* evil?
How do You feel *all* our sorrows,
multiplied billions of heartaches, agonies, pains,
and not collapse, implode?

O triune God,
Your power and strength
bear it *all*
beyond any comprehension.

Crushed on the cross
but not annihilated
Triune unity strengthened Jesus in His hour.

O Three in One,
You are eternal, forever
Alpha and *Omega*.

And You pray for me, Jesus, Holy Spirit!
You love me, will strengthen me!
Little, insignificant dust-to-dust me.

Such *knowledge* is wonderful to me.
I fall before You
and worship Your majesty.
Worthy is the Lamb!

AMEN.

ONE DAY I unexpectedly bumped into a woman I knew but hadn't seen in some time. I expected a pleasant encounter but instead was met with an accusation that stabbed my character, my integrity.

I was shocked and hurt at her hasty conclusion. Was the history and context of my life nothing? Living rightly has always been a high value of mine. I know I'm not perfect. Who is?

There was no "Help me understand," only words that felt judgmental and shook me to my core.

The day I wrote this prayer, I took my wound, my friends' wounds, the horrors of another school shooting that week, the memory of the joke the men enjoyed at my expense, and the burdens of others to my Father, who knows all our hearts.

I realized as the words filled the page that I now knew how the psalmist felt when he poured forth words of despair over betrayals, losses, and confusion over God's apparent distance. I understood too a tiny taste of what Jesus felt, knew, and experienced at the hands of so many who did not know who He was. And I thanked Him for that glimpse, that fellowship of His suffering, uniting me to Him ever more closely, leading me to more worship and adoration.

May this be true of you too.

May you always take your wounds, your hurts, your agonies to the only One who can bring peace and hope in unspeakably hard circumstances.

Isaiah 53:4, 6; Revelation 21:6; Psalm 139:6

NINETEEN
Sabbath

O Giver of love
and all that is good,
You have provided Sabbath
for me,
calendar marked since the dawn of time
for me.

Oh, how I needed rest in my mommy years;
we practiced Sabbath,
knew You made this holy day
for me
my personal gift it seemed.
Saying no to normal on Sunday
protected
gave rest and life.

Oh, how I need rest today in these sandwich years
children gone, parents aging
easier to ignore Sabbath now
no little eyes watching
so much work to be done in this season,
so little time.

Often we, Your children,
think Your Old Testament admonitions
archaic, outdated.
You shall keep the *Sabbath* holy.
What's wrong with a Sunday run to the grocery store?
A quick trip to the mall?
Sunday practices for our kids' teams?

Nothing, inherently,
but doing the ordinary can tarnish the holy.
Ignoring His intentions
declares I know better.

Sabbath is rhythm
the stability of constancy
the weekly celebration of the resurrection
a day to rejoice in redemption
and rest
never for legalism.

In music there are rests,
for balance in harmony, crescendo, conclusion.
In painting, planned spaces for calming neutrals,
pauses for the eye,
balance for color intensity.

Rising bread must rest
Night was made for rest
Winter another ordained pause for rest
Our fallen-from-perfection bodies need rest.
This need reminds me of my limits, finitude,
my every breath a reliance on Thee.

Rest is sacred,
its practice declared holy,
but we doers can't imagine
change . . . work . . .accomplishment
in rest, in sleep, yet
He gives to His *beloved* even in his sleep.

Lord, my life is full of good things
but I often try too much;
we moderns
foolishly fill calendars to the brink,
evenings, before-dawn risings,
weekends jammed, pace frantic,
minimal margins, few boundaries,
paltry pauses, rare days of rest.

Your words are life,
wisdom, guidance, health.

You gave me Sabbath for *my good*
my rest
for our collective good, Your children.

By keeping it I bow before Your eternal wisdom
and declare
I am
ever Yours, my God.
Honoring Your rhythms
choosing to keep Sabbath
honors You.

Thank You for this gift of rest,
which I need more than I know.

AMEN.

Exodus 20:8; Psalm 127:2 NASB

TWENTY

Disappointed with God

I feel as if You don't see what's happening,
that perhaps You don't care we are experiencing this.
I know differently, know the truth,
still believe, embrace the truth.
But I can't feel any assurance of Your
presence at this moment.

I have felt this kind of disappointment before,
this is not the first time,
so I should have a backup, some verse that worked before.
But I feel just as bewildered as every other time.

I'm really trying to live for You
I'm working hard to make a difference in people's lives
I'm not wasting my life with things
You list in Your Word as bad.

Living for You feels really hard.
It's hard work, full of plagues of all kinds,
people who disappoint and fail,
ideas that seem like good ones
that even seem blessed by You
but fall flat.

Nothing seems easy in the Christian life right now.
Nothing.
Not surrender, not faith, not prayer, not
peace or Your promised rest.
What am I missing, Lord?
Show me what You want me to see,
to learn, to know.

Your Word tells me
whoever *believes* in Him will not be disappointed.
I see now
I am believing what is false about You,
thinking You "should" reward me.
I am disappointed because I did not hope in You alone.
You never disappoint
But life in this broken world often does.

I spent my life serving my husband and kids.
Now, I thought, is my time to make a difference
in the larger world.
But it's not working, not like I expected.

This setback feels like a slammed door,
a season-ending injury.
I don't want to just survive
I want to thrive!

Many who don't love You seem to be thriving
making tons of money
reaching lots of people with their ideas.
Some ideas seem temporal to me;
my vision is to make Your name known.
Today, it seems to be wrecked.

O Lord God
What do I do?
What do You want?
What is Your plan?
I just wish You'd return so I could
be done with all the trials.

Deliver me and make Your way clear
Guide me today
no matter what tomorrow may bring.

AMEN.

MANY TIMES IN this recent season of transition, change, and starting over, I was surprised by disappointment. In hindsight, I suppose I shouldn't have been. It is my nature to underestimate how long, how much, or how hard a project, a recovery, a task will be, and this season was no exception.

But on one particular day, a day that promised hope and a brighter future, news came that completely knocked the wind out of our sails. I felt blindsided.

In my flesh, I always want to blame, to find someone or something at which to direct my "righteous" anger. But He reminds me there is so much more going on than what I can see or know. He calls me to surrender every day. It's the essence of faith, after all.

As the day this prayer was written unfolded, I remembered by His Spirit's whisper that I'm living in a world full of imperfect people—including me—who make mistakes, most not intentionally. Not everyone has the same values and standards that I do. And it's okay.

He also reminded me I am limited and can't do all things. I have to settle for less. In today's world, less is ridiculed.

I thanked Him and chose to trust Him with the mess we had to deal with, which was not of our own doing. It was an opportunity to show grace and love and generosity, knowing we would desire the same if the mistake was our own.

Are you facing a mistake made by someone you trusted that is now costing you? Do you feel the whole world is being disrupted, turned upside down?

May you give thanks with me for His overruling control, for His power to bring good out of even the worst mistakes, and for the opportunity to choose to be like Jesus in a hard place so that He might be pleased by your faith!

Romans 10:11 NASB

TWENTY-ONE

Learning Your Voice

My ear is tuned,
recognizes instantly the sound
of my husband, my children,
each unique timbre a comfort and joy.

Other voices known:
my mother, brothers, older grands, many many friends,
each unique, each familiar.

Your voice, my Lord,
my closest Friend,
no audible sound, harder to recognize.

Your decibels a heart whisper,
a sudden knowing,
a reminder of truth,
an illumination of verse, of words,
a peace,
an assurance.

All as clear as if spoken aloud;
Your voice, words, language
from another realm

written by the One who walks on water.

In my intuition,
my spirit, my heart, my soul,
I hear You,
my inner ear knows Your sound.
"My sheep hear My *voice* . . ."

An inner confirmation, this is the treatment,
"Yes, go here, follow this idea.
This is of Me."

I hear You in Your Word.
The time I asked, "Should I get a face lift?"
Your Spirit spoke clearly within,
"Lay up *treasures* in heaven."
Yes, Lord.

Identity changed
from mom to empty nest.
I asked, "Who am I now?"
You replied,
"I am *with* you."

Words of affirmation
of truth spoken by friends who belong to You,
"You are the most persevering woman I know"

are also Your words
of love and belief from Your heart to mine
through another.

Your Spirit within
inspires my creativity,
plants desires, dreams that fulfill Your good works
prepared before the foundation of the world.

But not all opportunities, ideas
are from You.
Another mimics Your speech;
the one who vied for Jesus' subjugation in the desert
whispers suggestions, stokes desires,
seeks to lure from following Jesus.

I'm learning with length of days
to recognize Your silent yet audible voice;
it never contradicts Grace and Truth.

Less dramatically but no less surely
You lead me and guide me
as You did the early apostles.

Sometimes You close the way ahead
make my journey winding and arduous,
like Paul's missionary voyages.

I don't like my way being blocked,
I bring my complaint to You,
You remind me the delays are of You.
Will I trust You?

You have opened my eyes to see You
as You are
not as I have imagined.

More than ever in my life, Lord God,
I want to hear Your voice
to know Your clear leading in my life.

Give me ears to hear,
grow my perception, tune my hearing,
and most of all
give me eager anticipation as I wait
on Your timing,
Your answers, Your guidance.

AMEN.

John 10:27; Matthew 6:20; Isaiah 4:10

TWENTY-TWO
Favorites

My kids have all said it,
in singsong-y voices,
"The youngest is the favorite."
I can still hear the refrain.

I resisted their words in my heart
knowing I love them, all six,
the same.

Isn't that true, Lord?

Perhaps it was idealism,
to believe I loved all equally,
thinking more *highly* of myself, my ability, than I ought.
I thought that was part of my job
as mom;
love each one the same.

But now, Lord, I see,
I didn't love 100 percent equally then,
don't . . . can't even now,
for who can measure or know but You, Lord?

I understand today
only God who is perfect can love perfectly,
equally, without favoritism.
You tell us, "Do not show *partiality*."
You know I tried hard, Lord,
to be fair, treat each one equally in love.

Even though my love is flawed, imperfect,
I do love all deeply
with admiration and affection for each uniqueness,
for their varied gifts, strengths, obstacles overcome,
with thanksgiving for
every step of faith,
every gift of forgiveness,
every step toward Jesus.

One a warrior, fights for others,
for causes, for relationships.
Another a carpenter, builder with wood and words.
A third rescued creatures in youth, children as an adult.

Our dreamer has found identity in You;
our high ACT tester negotiates deals,
relationships, leads well;
our giggler is loving and leading a gaggle of kids.

All six fashioned by You
for *good works* prepared by You beforehand
for Your purposes and plans.

Watching the unfolding of these lives,
the addition of spouses, children, lifestyle choices,
the roads of their life journeys
so unlike ours;
they answer now to You, Lord,
not us.
We watch and pray with patience for the process,
prayer for the work of Christ in each heart.

In my fallenness, Lord,
some personalities, life stages, choices are easier
to love, enjoy, embrace, and admire.
We are all broken,
my children are fragile clay pots too.

Today the "favorite" is the one I'm with.
None are under our roof or in our town,
so our visits are immersions.
We enter their orbits
glimpse and taste the work You are doing
in each one

in each spouse
in each child.

It is a marvel to watch
to support, encourage, and know how to pray.

May I love each of my favorites with Your love, Jesus,
for mine is always imperfect.

AMEN.

Romans 12:3; James 2:1; Ephesians 2:10

TWENTY-THREE

Christmas Card Photos

It's a lovely tradition
going back decades of years
my grandfather in his properly starched uniform
a black-and-white photo printed "Merry Christmas"
sent home from India
during the war.

Our first Christmas
we sent a photo, the two of us,
me wrapped in a bright orange coat,
my husband in '70s plaid
bundled against beautiful Boulder snow.

This tradition repeated annually
over forty-plus years
to share our family with yours
to show how we've all grown
to wish you and yours hope and happiness

Patience, time, repeated "Say cheese,"
parental bribing, threats,
eventually a smiling,

even perfectly peaceful image emerges.

Never displayed on the photos we send,
the arguments, 'tudes, gritted teeth,
our collective ugly brokenness—
mine,
my husband's,
our children's

Though I hoped and prayed my family
would all love each other
like our photos portray,
offenses have been suffered
creating discomfort among siblings
and more pain than I imagined for us parents.

I understand the lyrics penned by Longfellow,
"'There is no peace on earth,' I said;
'For hate is strong,
And mocks the song
Of peace on earth, good-will to men!'"[7]

Nothing hurts like family hurt.
Wounded lambs, wandering sheep
Chicks who refused to be gathered
Pain piercing a parent's heart.

Little disagreements, big misunderstandings
become seeds of distance, discomfort
when children grow up.
Family geography widens as these now young adults
choose their own values, careers, finances,
parenting styles, school choices,
church choices.

We are not alone.
Every grown-up family I know suffers loss,
passive-aggressive behaviors,
depressions, woundedness, pride,
failure to forgive
holding on to hurts
the ideal of siblings as adult best friends
too uncommon.

Dysfunctional relationships the norm
not the exception in the body of Christ.
God's children, His family,
all sinners, all broken, all imperfect yet saved by grace,
connected by blood and adoption.

Even the perfect Parent does not have perfect kids;
all of us have rebelled, gone *astray*,

still learning grace, mercy, peace
from You and toward one another.

Even biblically grounded moms and dads
cannot avoid damaging, can't perfectly protect.
our ever-present sin nature both unites and divides us.

And so our family mirrors His.

Beautiful Savior,
announced on Christmas morn,
born a sacrifice for Eden's shattered mirrors,
only You can transform hearts
heal hurts
resurrect relationships
restore all that sin has stolen.

This Christmas season, O God,
bring revival to my heart,
for it is in me
where change must begin.

My goal must always be Your glory and fame
not a Christmas photo to be admired.

One day our smiling faces will be authentic
perfectly reflecting the joy we now pretend too often
at Christmas.

"Then pealed the bells more loud and deep:
'God is not dead nor doth He sleep;
The Wrong shall fail,
The Right prevail,
With peace on earth, good-will to men.'"[8]

Come quickly, Lord Jesus.

AMEN.

Isaiah 53:6

TWENTY-FOUR

Why Me?

From before the foundation of the world,
more romantic than any fairy tale
is His choosing me
to be His own!

I am ever His,
He is
ever mine!

But I have learned my true nature . . .
and now seeing it as it is . . .
how could my flawed, sin-infected, self-absorbed
being have any value to Him?
It is beyond comprehension.

Why, Lord,
why would You want me?

There is no inherent good in me,
for You declare
there is *none* who seeks after God
none who is righteous

none who does good
not even *one*.
Your absolute declaration should be
the end of the story.
It makes no sense
Your desire for me.

But the fairy tales are right.

There is a Prince
One who sees
beauty in me
a beast, a rebel,
a Cinderella.

This Prince knows my name
He calls me
tells me I am his own
has given me a ring of promise
covered me with His sparkling coat
of righteousness, purity.

Inestimable Grace and Love
had compassion on my irretrievably lost state.
You longed to show me perfect love

lavishly gifted me with redemption
made me fit to receive You!

Again this knowledge . . .
incomprehensible
leaves me wordless
silences me in awe.

Promises upon more promises have You left for me
including my favorite,
Your promised return for me one day,
to take me Home
to the place You are preparing
especially designed for me.
Because You know me intimately,
it will be beautiful and perfect beyond my imagining.

Until then You live within me,
I belong to You.
Your name is *near*, my Emmanuel.
My heart is Your home,
my body Your temple.

You are transforming me into Your likeness,
writing a story about You with my life,
a letter to be read by many,

written not with *ink* but with the Spirit of God
on the tablet of my heart.

May You always feel at home in me, Lord.
Unite my heart to fear Your name
for You are my strength and my portion *forever*.

I can't wait to see You face to face!

Amen.

Romans 3:10–12; Psalm 75:1; 1 Corinthians 3:3; Psalm 86:11; 73:26

TWENTY-FIVE

To Be Beautiful

It was seventh grade, I think,
when I first wanted to be beautiful.
By high school I was aware of looking my best for photos
already knew which was my "best side"
checked my makeup and hair at every bathroom break.

The desire of every woman
to be admired for her God-fashioned beauty
made for good in the beginning.

Unless her beauty is abused by cruelty
and her God-given glory is crushed,
making the most of what God has designed
for His honor and glory
is still good.

But the Tempter . . .
most beautiful and intelligent of all the angels . . .
decided he was worthy of worship
and he calls me to follow his lead
to succumb to my *own* pride
to be noticed for my *own* honor

my *own* praise
as if I alone created my visage.

It is an eternal trap
we rich modern consumers relentlessly pursue—
paparazzi- and Instagram-worthy
pay any amount to sculpt, trim, and perfect—
but have no idea
"what beauty of soul might be."[9]

True lasting beauty is deeper than skin,
seen in men and women on fire for the King,
who live for Him above all else,
who count this world as nothing
compared to *knowing* Him.

Magnetic Mother Teresa, followed by thousands,
not for her wrinkled face, humble tunic, head scarf.
But her soul shone forth from a face reflecting glory,
her all-surrendered heart,
selfless love for the least of these,
she captivated the world.
Her diminutive *form* declared she had been with Jesus.

Makeup companies promise women radiance at any age
but all are lies,

for radiance only comes from within . . .
a reflection of the face of God.
Those who look to Him are radiant . . .
Then you shall see and be *radiant*.

The more I seek You, Lord,
the more I will be purified from sin's de*form*ity,
and beauty of soul will grow within
even as my outer beauty fades away.

Therefore I live with great hope.
One day soon You will trans*form* my lowly body
to be like Your *glorious* body!

May my heart always be hungry for Your beauty
over my own.

May I desire the loveliness of Christ
more than the external beauty money can buy.
May I love Your image, Your face more than my own.

May I live for future glory and radiance
not for today's fleeting momentary pleasure
which distracts from knowing You deeply.

Amen.

Philippians 3:8; Psalm 34:5; Isaiah 60:5; Philippians 3:21

TWENTY-SIX

Suffering in Marriage

Marriage to a difficult man
happens in all marriages.

Life is hard;
depressions, insecurities, verbal volleys,
overlooked at work, suddenly fired,
choosing sin, feeling isolated or alone;
any man can be difficult
when life is hard.

Sometimes a husband's decision to change jobs,
make an investment,
hire this person, fire that one
costs friendships, sows fears, anxieties.
Delaying decisions sometimes just as hard
as no decisions at all.

So, Lord,
which is harder . . . leading or following?
We women assume leading is the easier
but there are risks in every step of leadership
just as there are risks in every step of following.

Like Peter
we are prone to compare our lot,
what You chose for us.

On the beach after their post-resurrection breakfast,
You asked Peter to feed and take care of Your sheep,
asked Him if He loved You,
told him one day he would be led away.
Instead of answering Jesus . . . Peter deflected,
"What about him?" pointing at John.
Jesus replied, "You follow Me."

I am so like Peter.
I look at everyone else, look at my husband too,
and assume his lot is easier,
I got the harder life.
Like Eve, I too easily believe You shortchanged me.

You have made it clear my first responsibility
is to follow You
and Your plan for me,
which includes following my husband
as he seeks, tries to follow You.
Of course You don't want me or any wife
to follow him into sin
or enable false living.

"You follow Mc"
means I study Your Word seriously
to know You as You really are
not as I imagine You to be.

"You follow Me"
means I learn from You
how to be the wife you want me to be
for my husband, for no two are alike.

"You follow Me"
means to be exemplary in love and respect,
especially when times are hard,
knowing my example can lead him to You
just as Esther did her godless husband.

Oneness in all decisions isn't always possible
and so wives must learn to give it all to Jesus
then wait, pray, trust, pray, believe that He sees,
He knows all.
God is our *Husband* . . . He promised to take care of us.

You, my Lord, always know
who is right and who is wrong.
You know my sufferings,
You know the end from the beginning

and all You desire to work in me, in us,
as I trust You . . . daily.

Until this marital storm is past,
help me to remember You are near us both.

May my heart cling to this truth:
"Christ within us, Christ among us,
Christ the first and Christ the last,
Love incarnate, hold Your children,
Till the storm of life is past."[10]

AMEN.

Isaiah 54:5

TWENTY-SEVEN

Sex

Well, Lord, I, um,
want to talk to You about sex.
Again.

You know this has been an ongoing adjustment
in our decades of marriage.
You know the number of multiplied misunderstandings,
how vastly different we are.

In our early years
miscommunication, learning one another,
baggage from the past, the culture, the church,
birth-control issues,
youthfulness a help and a hindrance.

Our middle years were harder,
pregnancies, loss of sleep, nighttime feedings,
fatigue, emotional needs,
menstrual cramps, real headaches, awful allergies,
a million distractions and then . . .
teens who create drama . . . How do
you transition to sex from that?
And did I mention fatigue, Lord?

Our nest emptied and we thought ease would come,
but I underestimated . . . more fatigue
. . . from prodigal years,
discovered patterns of past survival skills
needed midcourse corrections.

I remember talking to You often,
asking for heart change, real growth in our sex life,
for smooth seas now that we were alone.

As usual for me, Your answer, Your changes
came not as I wanted, nor as quickly as I desired.
After all, You aren't
a fairy godmother waving a magic wand.

I am impatient.
And I have learned I will never arrive
at mastery in any area while a traveling pilgrim.

More repair work was needed,
more growth in relationship and in appreciation,
but slowly, because we didn't quit,
imperceptibly, like the upward growth of an oak,
we became stronger, healthier, more secure than ever.

And one day I heard Your whisper, Lord.
From suffering to sex

from abasement to accomplishment
all experiences are vain . . . empty . . . meaningless
when divorced from the One
who knows the plans He has for me.

You know me, Lord.
Meaning matters to me . . . in my soul;
it was transcendence for which I longed,
for our experience to be more mutually meaningful.
It was not technique this time, though
sometimes that is needed,
nor another book, though some are urgently necessary.
But for us, at this season, it was You we needed most.

We began to regularly invite You into our intimacy
to talk to You as one,
to thank You for our differences,
for the plans You have for us,
remembering nothing is impossible with You;
repeated surrender to You . . . Your presence,
deeper meaning emerged, more rest.

Thank You that Your resurrection power
can continually bring new life to sex
as we bring it to You,
invite You in,

follow Your individualized leading,
and wait patiently for You to bring the growth.

Thank You too that one day
Your mysterious plans and purposes for sex,
beyond bearing children,
will be known, make perfect sense.
One day we will all understand Your good design.

There is rich, beautiful significance in sex,
this enigma of Your creation.
I praise You for this gift to us in our marriage.
Even in our later years.

AMEN.

TWENTY-EIGHT
Beauty Beckons

You have taught me, Lord, that beauty is not
just in the eye of the beholder,
but is transcendent even in matter,
seen in an infinity of
forms formed by You.

The shape, *form*, of a flower
the figure, or *form*, of a face, the human body,
musical and literary *forms*,
the inner root, or *form*, that germinates
exterior traits including shape, size, and color.

You, my God,
are the divine Artist,
the endlessly imaginative Creator
calling me to see reflections of You,
hints of Your glory
in every glint of beauty.

Because I'm made like You,
with intellect, emotions, a heart to worship,
I can notice, feel wonder, am enriched by the beautiful
which leads me to adore and love You.

A lion, a kitten, or any other animal
has no capacity to stare enraptured at a sunset
to marvel at the sound of Mozart
to gather a bouquet of roses.

Our pets are not like us
no matter how much they delight.
Only Adams and Eves perceive beauty,
know it is a reflection of You.

Beauty points to You
to Your supreme genius, nobility, purity, and truth,
while ugliness, the damaging of the pure *form*,
becomes de*form*ed,
dulls our capacity wonder, to love.

Sin, choosing my way over Yours, de*forms* too,
is always pro-my-choice
inevitably leads to pain, ugliness, jadedness,
dulls my ability to be alive to beauty.
When Jesus was made sin . . . for me . . . for us,
it is written, he had no *beauty* or *form*.

But You have promised
good can come from any evil, any sin, any ugliness.
The cross defies even the worst evil
displays like a jewel victorious overcoming

by the inherent power of His perfection
the ultimate Beauty.

Repentance is therefore beautiful
because it is a return
to Your lovely, pure Way for me.
When I am not conformed to this *world*,
refuse the lure, the bait to self,
then I can be transformed, my *mind* renewed,
*form*ed more like You.

This is the call of beauty to my soul:
renounce my pro-self ways, unveil my face,
that I may behold Your glory
as You metamorphose me into Your likeness.

Thank You, my God,
for giving me a love for beauty
for delighting me with numberless *form*s of wonder
which lead to a growing fascination with You,
the supreme Beloved.
Thank You for drawing me to more of You,
for "anything less than Everything
is *now* simply not enough."[11]

A M E N.

Isaiah 53:2; Romans 12:2

TWENTY-NINE
Borrowing

Lord, I need to borrow something.

We had another disagreement,
my husband and I.
His officing at home for a year now
has produced more opportunities
to trust You than I expected.
Exposed more of my flaws than I care to see.

My time is not my own,
my house is no longer my daytime sanctuary,
my kitchen island his landing strip.
Like when my children
usurped my world, my space, my peace.

I remind myself
I'd rather have him and his messes
than not have him at all,
this house is OURS
not mine.

Again I pray,
thank You, Lord, that I don't live alone.

I am so very grateful.
I know Your sufficiency would be enough
for a life of widowhood;
thank You that the time has not yet come.

But today, Lord, I am in need.
I need to borrow
(though I won't return, can't repay)
from Your divine nature
because You promised
Your divine *power* offers me
everything for life and *godliness*!

Oh, how I need everything You offer, Lord!

In myself I'm so aware
I can't produce good responses
don't have patience
can't manufacture godliness
or self-control or perseverance
or love.

Because You know this,
You invite me to come to Your throne room,
ask for what I lack,
walk up to Your banquet table and take all I need

from every inexhaustible platter,
every overflowing fountain of pure drink!

Amazing Grace,
You have set before me
unending supplies of divine nature.
Whoever will may *come*.
Before Your table I bow and say grace.

Help me feed on You always.
Fill me with Your love, for mine is inadequate.
Grant me Your patience, grace, and every other virtue,
for I lack them all.

For Your happiness and delight
in giving to me,
it pleases Your Father's heart to touch mine,
and because You command me,
I ask:
Fill me, O my Savior,
with the riches of Your divine nature.

AMEN.

Recently I had a dream.

Like many dreams, it was strange and made no sense. I saw a very large crowd of people milling among vibrantly colored awnings, beneath which were displayed multiple hundreds of various items. Vendors were shouting and waving their arms with their wares raised high for all to see. Pennants were snapping in the wind. Strings of bells jingled on tentpoles, adding to the cacophony of notes.

Standing behind the tents, but still among the people, was a man. He didn't have a lavishly appointed display, but he too was offering something. As I watched all the activity, I noticed one person approach him. He showed the stranger what he carried but I couldn't see it. Not long after, I saw another join them. And then another.

The man began to walk away and the three followed. Others joined. Following his circuitous path, they disappeared behind doorways, reappeared in alleys, then turned a corner and again vanished. I sensed a magnetism about this stranger because of the way the others followed him. I was increasingly intrigued by what he was carrying because this mysterious something remained obscured, not waved aloft like all the other hawkers' wares.

I woke up.

And I knew. The man had been with Jesus, and that experience, that transformative "something about him" was what drew the others to follow him and leave the other vendors' cheap counterfeit trinkets behind.

I remembered Acts 4:13: "Peter and John . . . were uneducated, common men. . . . And [the people] recognized that they had been with Jesus."

I wondered, *Do others see that unexplainable something in me? Do those around you see you have been with Jesus?* It's what I want now more than ever: to be with Jesus, to experience His presence more and more, and for it to change my life so it's obvious . . . I have been with Him.

Partaking of His divine nature, which is promised to us, is the potion of transformation. Have you ever considered how stunningly generous it is of Almighty God to condescend, to stoop down to me and you, and to share His godly qualities? Our pride tells us we "should" be able to be more patient or gentle or fill-in-the-blank. Seeing my absolute bankruptcy of virtue is as wise as looking a cancer diagnosis squarely on and saying yes to treatment. Ignoring either can be deadly.

The longer I walk with God the more I see how right is His declaration, "No one seeks for God. . . . No one does good, not even one" (Romans 3:11–12). Instead of trying harder, I invite you to join me in taking from God's limitless supply of divine nature.

Let's be women who run to Him with all our inabilities and partake of His "everything for life and godliness." Then those around us—our spouses, families, friends, neighbors, and even strangers—will see that we have been with Jesus!

May it be so for each one of us, Lord!

---

2 Peter 1:3; Revelation 22:17

THIRTY

Do You Want to Get Well?

Puzzling, Lord,
are the questions You asked.

To the invalid man
who had lived in his unnamed condition
for thirty-eight years,
You asked, of all things,
"Do you *wish* to get well?"
What kind of question is that?
Of course someone sick for that long
would want to be healed, right?

Jesus, You know all things.
Did You see something we didn't?
Were You inviting him
to something more needed than physical health?
Were You testing his faith?
You who looks on the *heart*,
what did You see?

Sometimes I want to feel sorry for myself,
to remain depressed for having been hurt,
wronged through "no fault of my own,"
I am quick to assume.
Other times I've relished my anger,
feeling justified, superior over this one
who does not deserve to be loved.

Maybe Jesus was seeing inside the man's heart
a victim mentality,
and that is what mattered most
to Jesus,
not his physical disability.

My gentle Savior,
how often do I sit by the Bethesda pool
waiting for someone
some book
some plan
to help me get well
instead of looking, running to You?

Lord, why do we hang on to our pains?
To gain attention,
to be pitied,
hoping for love?

How can I forget You looked on me with compassion
from the cross?
You have pulled me up
from the prison beside the pool.
I have been bought.
I am Yours!

What do You see in me today
that You want to heal?
What pains, shames, guilts from the past
are You waiting for me to give You?
What jail door are You eager to open today?

I am unworthy, Lord.
But You want to set me free because You love me!
Give me eyes to see what makes me lame
then help me fix my eyes on You,
the Author and Finisher of my faith.

Help me daily celebrate
my great redemption story!
For You called me by name,
lifted me up,
and have been healing me ever since.
AMEN.

John 5:6 NASB; 1 Samuel 16:7

THIRTY-ONE
Surrender

In Your story, Jesus, I read,
"I can do *nothing* on My own initiative."
Nothing!
Not one word spoken,
no healing, no sermon, no decision
on Your own initiative.

Not because You couldn't
but because You wouldn't.
To act on Your own would have ruined the plan.

Your words stun me.
I shake my head
in disbelief,
yet I know it's true.

Five times You repeated these exact words
many more the concept
of complete surrender
to Your Father's preordained plan.
Your repetition, an echo, a symphonic refrain,
magnetic notes pulling me to You.

How many times a day do I speak
on my own initiative
act on my own initiative
share how I really feel about so and so
on my own initiative?

Simply stunning
is the truth that You lived every moment
in absolute, unwavering surrender.
I cannot imagine, sadly,
being that united to the will of the Father.

But I know it's my calling too,
our intended design as women and men,
to become more like Jesus
to live more like He did
following His example of absolute surrender.

How easily I am consumed,
driven by my own desires
preoccupied by my own feelings, goals, plans.
When I awake each morning
to greet You before my eyes open
to offer my life to You at day's start
is not yet a perfected daily habit.

But it is my heart's desire;
more and more
my soul longs to be ever united with You, Jesus,
to walk as You walked with Your Father.
This togetherness can be mine
here on earth
always available for my choosing.

So . . . once again
for the thousandth-upon-thousandth time
I surrender all.
"All to Thee, my blessed Savior,
I surrender all."[12]

Help me remember,
do nothing on my own initiative,
instead
daily, hourly breathe breath prayers:
Thy will be *done*
fill me with Your Spirit
grant me all that I lack
in this moment and the next,
and the next.

AMEN.

THIRTY-TWO

Aging

I was young, naïve, invincible
promised myself at eight
I'd never get old.

In the Jesus Movement revival
I met Him, at nineteen,
learned He was soon to return
convinced I'd never be married, be a mom, or get old,
so imminent was Jesus' second coming.

But the nevers came.
Marriage
Babies
Age
Surprise baby at thirty-five
with five in tow, my exhaustion overwhelming.
My body had changed, no longer my own.

A crisis of faith, identity, before forty.
Dreams born in revival zeal—
to speak, be a woman of prayer,
do ministry, paint for His glory—

all shelved, let go
for the greater good of my six little disciples.

We do not lose *heart*,
I read that fortieth year.
Though my outer self is wasting away . . .
my inner life is being *renewed* day by day!
O God! You. Know. Me!

You see me invisibly toiling within these walls!
Same tasks, same instructions, same reminders,
repeat.
Endlessly, mind numbingly, impatiently.
My most important goal and prayer:
Will my children follow You?
Will they catch the truth, see you in our home?

It was . . . is . . . all for *your* sake,
the daily care of these people You gave.
I trusted You, depended on You,
accepted Your timing, Your plan,
chose to believe each day seen by You,
knowing my dreams might never be fulfilled tomorrow.
That too was . . . is . . . in Your hands.

Afflictions physical, emotional, relational
came in hard in my forties and fifties,
my soul broken but not crushed.
My clay pot cracked again and again and again,
but intact.

Gladly I have chosen to follow You
in the way up that is down,
with these never-imagined companions—
flabby arms, changing eyesight, endless fatigue—
but most important my beautiful children,
all now belong to You.

Days now a gift
not a right.
Lord, You know tomorrow can bring future fears;
being debilitated, set aside
can arrive at any age
if You so choose.
Only You know if cancer cells are lurking undetected.

Help me live today,
confident in Your presence,
knowing You are already ahead of me, in my future,
all that is hidden to me
is perfectly clear to You.

May Your Light shine forth
from this chosen vase of Your presence.
May I ever value
holy unseen work
over temporal health, achievement.

This light *momentary* affliction
of aging is for me
preparing an eternal weight of *glory.*

Help me embrace Your unique way for me,
today and every gifted day.

A MEN.

2 Corinthians 4:15–17

THIRTY-THREE
Marys and Soul Sisters

True love is brave
courageous, willing to risk, sacrifice;
and so three Marys, Salome, Joanna, and others
walked in the predawn darkness
to the tomb.

Why did they go?
Was it mere duty, a woman's obligation?
Perhaps one had signed up
for that morning's anointing work
but more than six said, "I'm coming too."

And why were there no men,
no brothers, no disciples, no secret Sanhedrin believers?
Were they kept away by the facts?
Jesus was really dead?
Death is final.
End of story.

Was devotion the motivation for this band of women?
Because He had changed their lives
they still loved Him

wanted to express their deep gratitude
even though He was gone?

But . . . is there more to see?
Is there something about us as women to notice?
Belief is a feminine noun, so . . .
do females have a different capacity for faith?
Perhaps even greater?
Eve did believe the deceiver first.

Because of love
the women went . . . just to be near Jesus.
That, for them, was enough.

And because of their devotion
they encountered angels!
Were rewarded . . . the first to recognize . . . see Jesus alive!
First to believe in His resurrection!

By contrast the men
stayed back
their love turning cold,
evaluating next steps to a new way forward, a new plan,
later rebuked by Jesus for not believing the women.

Would I have volunteered to go with the women,
to be near Jesus when all hope was lost?

My Jesus,
I want to be like these women
when my world feels hopeless,
my prayers lifeless,
to still desire to go near You.

I want to be quick to recognize Your unseen presence
respond with quick-to-believe faith
that rises above my fears.

Like these women,
when I give You my belief in obedience,
in surrender, in hope,
even as I wait for Your timing,
I am given life
by the Spirit of Him who *raised* Jesus from the dead.

I want to be rewarded for my faith
not rebuked for my unbelief.
May it be so, my Jesus,
my Savior.

AMEN.

FOR SEVERAL YEARS I've been thinking about this mystery of *belief* being a feminine word in the Greek; about the women being first at the tomb, the first to believe, the first to see Him, the first to proclaim Him; and about the idea of being near Jesus today even though we cannot see Him as did these women. It's a topic deeper and richer than my little brain can plumb, but it's been intriguing and captivating nonetheless.

I first wrote about these women in the spring of 2015; their brief but remarkable stories have marked me as a woman ever since. I understand the driving desire to be near a beloved someone who is now gone, in heaven. We go to the graves, the markers of our loved ones to feel near them just as these women did two thousand year ago. We understand.

How do we go near Jesus today?

Practicing His presence is the definition of faith. Talk to Him all day long. Ask for His help, His wisdom, His guidance, His grace, His forgiveness, and His perfect love when ours is not enough. And thank Him often by faith for His presence, *especially* when you don't feel it.

This is faith at its essence. This is the kind of belief these women, our sisters in Christ, demonstrated.

Romans 8:11

THIRTY-FOUR
Traditions

Beautiful repetitions—
"We always bake these cookies,
celebrate this way"—
bind us together
give life and meaning
raise us above our more ordinary days.

Other patterns, attitudes,
like recipes
handed down from generation to generation,
bind and blind.

Family histories of oppression, abuse, mediocrity
tragic, not new,
so too church families, God's called ones
set apart to lead, to serve, to love, also fallen.

Oh, Lord, how have You endured
these slanders to Your name?
What did You see, think, Jesus,
as the priests in Your day bound themselves
to legalism over Love,

as they labored again on yet another Passover,
slaying and offering thousands of bleeding lambs
while You were bleeding for them
as You bled for me?

An unimaginable interruption . . . to duty, traditions . . .
invisible hands tore the massive temple curtain in half;
aghast, horrified, did everything stop?
Did tradition-soaked priests attempt to cover the opening
to the Holy of Holies as if You, God, were suddenly exposed,
naked for all to see . . .
as was Your Lamb, hanging lifeless
on the tree?

What did these illustrious, learned
perfection-driven robed men think, feel, fear
as they gaped at two crimson puddles
of fabric?

Rule-bound hearts passionately resist change.
The lure of legalism, universal.

I too have felt fear, panic, vulnerability
when You, Jesus, disrupted my traditions,
my preferred way of doing life.
I too have responded like Your temple priests

with high-control crisis management.

O Great Disrupter of all that keeps me from You,
help me look at every interruption,
see Your invisible hands
ripping apart that which I falsely trust.

O Love that will not stop,
help me welcome each moment of lost control
as another divine opportunity
to engage, trust, rest with You,
to discover You alive, calling me to more of You!

Your invitation ever present.
"*Come* to Me,"
You repeat thousands of times a day . . . to me . . .
to billions of lost tradition-bound souls on this orb.

May You increasingly hear from me,
Yes, Lord, I come to You.
Show me a new way:
Your way.

AMEN.

WE HUMANS HAVE a love-hate relationship with rules.

We love them because they give definition, curbs, guidelines, order, and even safety to our lives. God knows we need them. But we hate them for confining us when we want to soar beyond their constrictions and limits. So all of us rebel and break the rules, the established order. We are born rebellious.

Easter is the ultimate clash of us rule-bound rebels with the great rule-breaking Transcender! Jesus both fulfilled the law in every way and yet rose above it all by showing us the greater law of Love.

Because of our brokenness, our sin-sickness, we can't keep the law of Love; we need the governance of rules and laws to order our lives and world. One day all that will change when Jesus comes back to rule on earth with a new and perfect world order!

May you look at your own heart and ask, "How much like the priests am I? Am I trusting in my efforts to please God? What is my response when He tears down my hopes, my security as He did the priests' on Good Friday?"

Matthew 11:28

THIRTY-FIVE
Heaven

A gentle summer's eve
we walked, blanketed in perfect temps
balmy air lightly caressing our skin
seemingly random conversation
turned to imagining . . .
to our future in Your home.

Told him I dream of being able to sing on key
to dance and leap and run
worship with exuberance and endless joy
and never get tired.

I imagine
movie theaters showing in real time
the crossing of the Red Sea,
or maybe wrinkles in time will open
through which any who desire can marvel
at the sun standing still, watch when it moved backward,
witness resurrections,
taste manna falling from heaven daily.

Why not?
There will be no *night* there
Time as we know it will be no more.

You tell us we will be like Jesus
who ate with His disciples after the resurrection
but also vanished from sight, walked through walls;
and if He walked on water before resurrection
of course no problem after,
and so shall we be free from temporal restrictions.

Eye has not seen nor the heart of man *imagined*.
what God has *prepared* for those who love Him.
So help us, Lord,
to stretch, flex our imaginations,
to anticipate what we know will be true,
then go beyond, picture what we cannot yet see.

An alive mind is Your good gift.

With it we plan vacations, weddings, birthdays, holidays
imagine a semester's syllabus, a speech
foresee the victory, the outcome of our work
then plan endless details to micromanage.
We live in the future more than we are aware.

More important than planning,
anticipating an earthly event
of magnitude and importance
is our looking to, visualizing, and planning for
heaven.

The memory of my Savior,
Lamb of God, who takes away the sin of the world
saying, "I am going to prepare a place for you,"
gives me expectant *hope,*
and He's been gone preparing for me
for two thousand years!

This is my more-real-than-this-world future!

Lord, I fear I, we, Your children, are too comfortable here
too rooted, attached to terra firma
with houses and land and important responsibilities.

Have we paused long enough to ask:
If the King called today,
would we refuse to leave, ask for a raincheck,
as did those twice invited to the wedding feast?

Your parable, Jesus, revealed a harsh response.
The king, deeply disappointed, declared
the invited not worthy.

To his servants, "Go invite others,
fill the wedding hall."
Oh, Lord, I want to be watching,
ready when You call!

As an Olympian disciplines daily
repetitiously for the coming contest,
so too must I prepare for my future
which is more sure than my today.

Bring revival, Lord, to Your children,
Restore our hope of heaven.
May we remember Jesus' words:
"Be on the *alert* . . .
you be ready too";
and may we sing again in our churches
of our future home with You.

AMEN.

Revelation 22:5; 1 Corinthians 2:9; John 1:29; 14:3; Matthew 24:42–44

THIRTY-SIX

New Assignments

Like a new school year
with its anticipations—Who will be my teacher,
who will be in my class, who will be my friends?—
so has been my life, Lord,
with more changing roles than I ever imagined.

My name as wife, then mom
took getting used to.
Then it became comfortable . . . and I liked it.
The day my youngest went to school
hard silence greeted me as I stepped inside our front door.
How did home become lonely, empty . . . ?
I dropped to my knees and asked,
O Lord, what do You have for me next?

Becoming a mom of teens another role,
for my littles were now bigs
more independent as we let out the kite string
and I was needed less and less.
Then they were gone.

Who was I without them?
For twenty-eight years I'd been their director
orchestrating each beginning act
encouraging each one's talent, strengths
comforting after every fall
preparing each for their solo debut.

My empty-nest assignments
took years of time to feel new rhythms,
my new place in God's greater dance.

Now I'm one of the older ones,
looked to as a repository of wisdom, advice
and this too feels odd, disorienting.
How did this happen?
How did we, best friend and I, get here?

You, O Lord, rule the seasons of earth;
planting and *harvest*, summer
and winter, shall not *end*,
so You rule the seasons of my life.

As I fly higher
snuggle nearer to Your heart,
I know greater peace,
much more rest in Your good provision

for every season
for every new assignment.

Manna.
All that I need You will always provide.
Always enough for each day
because it is Your nature to give abundantly
to Your children who ask.

With You I smile at the future,
anticipate the journey,
because You are with me,
my Emmanuel, my Friend.

AMEN.

ANOTHER DREAM OF mine, this one vivid and oh so real as I awoke one February morning in the winter of 2017: I walked downstairs to my kitchen to get my coffee, and as I rounded the corner into the dining room, I was startled to see small white discs all over the floor. Scanning the room, I saw them sprinkled on the kitchen floor too.

I was curious, puzzled, intrigued. So I bent over to pick up one of the dime-sized rounds. And then because I thought of what it might be, I tasted it with my tongue. It was sweet, and I knew. It was manna!

At that moment I woke up.

I threw on my fleece and hurried downstairs for my coffee and my Bible. I looked up the verse, and I was right; manna was white, had a sweet taste, and was provided daily every morning.

We had just begun our voyage to a new horizon—transition from forty years of ministry to new yet unknown ministry. Already the water was choppier than expected, but in His great kindness God reminded me and us that He was not only with us but would daily give us bread. Sustenance for every unknown step ahead.

Though the memory of that dream has faded, the confidence in God's fatherly care of us has not wavered. No matter what uncomfortable unknown assignment you are facing, you can know that God will be with you and will care for your needs every single day.

It's who He is. He cannot stop loving you, caring for you, and providing for you.

May you too be comforted in this knowledge.

Genesis 8:22

THIRTY-SEVEN

Letting Go,
Holding Fast

We mamas love our babies,
cocoon them in blankets,
lullaby them to sleep,
feed, clothe, dote, nourish, help, guide;
it is good and right.

As young adults we become parents,
the comfort, warmth, safety of home
created for us or created by us for us
changes . . .
as parents we now create secure environments
for new little ones.

We discover abruptly
comfort, sleep, security
are not preeminent,
allegiances shift.
Letting. Go. Begins.

In the quiet dark of night
my fears led to a bargaining dialogue with God.
My newly in-love heart,
adoring weeks-old baby two,
asking the Sovereign One,
"What will his future be?"

Will he live to be five?
Silence.
Okay. Will I have him till he's twelve?
Silence.
Twenty, Lord?
Silence.
Seconds passed as my son continued to eagerly suck,
oblivious to my heart angst.

Finally I knew.
No length of years would be enough,
and God was kind enough to keep silent
waiting for me to let go
of my desire to control, to know.

Hold fast to Me, He said.

Multitudes of letting-go moments have filled my life,
releasing my chicks thousands of times to Your care.

Prying my fingers from hopes, dreams, goals
for each little one.

Surrendering plans, desires, dreams for my own life too,
influence, accomplishment, a name
all relinquished to You.

Letting go too of old ways of finding comfort
old habits of feigned dignity
patterns built to support self-confidence.

You strip me
leave me feeling exposed, raw, afraid;
but when I run to You,
instead of away,
I unclutch my self-made image,
self-designed plans
die to my desire to appear all together . . .
worthy . . . on my own.

Self-made systems crumble . . . when I see as You do,
Your love guides me
to clutch to Your side,
to cling to You alone.

And because I know You hold fast to me in love
I know You will deliver me;

so too will You protect me
because You know my name!

There is a day appointed
when I will let go of it all
forever
and so it is for everyone who has breath
no false pretenses or material things will go with us
when our time is up.

Until then I will choose the things that please You
and hold fast to Your way, Your *covenant*.
For You are my *life* and length of days.
Nothing else satisfies but You.

Hanging on more tightly than ever,

AMEN.

Psalm 91:14; Isaiah 56:4; Deuteronomy 30:20

THIRTY-EIGHT

Advent

The first promise of hope after the fall,
"Her *offspring* will bruise your head."
Eve, sure her firstborn was the promise fulfilled . . .
but Cain killed Abel,
her heart and hopes dashed, crushed . . .

But God . . .

Like breadcrumbs along the path
more hints, clues, promises sprinkled.
Deliverers, kings, prophets
but none the Messiah.

Though hope was deferred
waiting never ceased,
watching endured.

On the darkest of nights,
gathered crumbs became the Bread of Life
sent incognito that first Advent,
coalesced clues few knew;
even raising the dead
fed the narrative

until . . .
pooling blood beneath a cross
killed. all. waiting. hope.

He was.

First century . . . twenty-first century
gaps in the story filled
explained by the gospel
still the drumbeat continues
wait, watch, be alert . . .
keep Your lamp burning.

Christianity lives in Advent,
today the "Time Between"[13]
this present
bookended by Christmas Day and That Day.

We His temples
commissioned to go into all the world,
to teach, make disciples, bring His kingdom to earth
as it is in heaven;
to live cruciform lives,
shaped by His transforming dwelling in us
clay forms shining forth His beauty.

He is.

God's promises are sure;
it is impossible for Him to lie;
therefore
His second Advent. Will. Dawn.
Christ will return to judge, rule, and reign victoriously;
all will recognize Him
nothing will be concealed.

Sadly the church at large has fallen into lethargy;
the rapture didn't happen decades ago
may not happen, some say.
Disillusionment has led to complacency
to scoffing
as foretold by Peter.
Where is the *promise* of His coming?
All things continue as they have since *creation*.

Be watchful, be ready, be alert,
You repeated to Your disciples over and over
more breadcrumbs timed to Your certain steady drumbeat,
every word, every jot and tittle
will be fulfilled, You declared with
power and great authority!

He is to come!

Every step of faith
needs anticipation, expectation, hope
to be genuine faith;
counting the days, looking ahead
imagining what is yet to be,
we are redeemed for the here-and-now
and the yet-to-be.

O Lord, forgive our arrogance,
our confident enlightenment
our shallow temporal view of today;
there is so much we do not know.

Advent, a crucial theme of Your story:
Your patient waiting for all
who will to come to repentance,
our patient and eager waiting
for Your return for us.

I believe Your promises.
A second Advent is coming;
every December we remember
first promises of a Deliverer were fulfilled,
future promises will be too.

May we feed our anticipation
of Your soon return,

talk together with expectant joy,
even if our specific beliefs differ,
imagining seeing You face-to-face
is worthy conversation!

May we watch the news of our day
as depressing and frightening as it is
with eyes to see hints of Your plan being fulfilled;
You are there for those with eyes to see.
You are working, preparing the way
for Your second Advent,
even when we can't see,
as surely as You did Your first.

Advent's story will close
today's chapters will end
and another will begin.
And we will be with
our Alpha and Omega
forever!

Come quickly, Lord Jesus.

Amen.

Genesis 3:15; Revelation 1:8; 2 Peter 3:4

THIRTY-NINE

The Incarnation

A gossamer veil
between this world and the next,
division of temporal and eternal
seen and unseen . . .
Pierced.

Light of the world
sent by God,
broke through . . .
Came to us.

Emptied
became microscopic
passed the curtain to our side . . .
Entered the chosen cell.

From that other world—
more real, substantive than eye can see
where angels dwell
battle, worship
do Your every bidding
shining with the light of Your glory—

He came!

On this side of the veil
women know birth
the pain, agony, utter humiliation.
Did Mary fear for her life, expect her own death
as she pushed
the eternal Son of God,
Son of the *Most High*,
through her birth canal
bleeding forth new life?

Was she utterly depleted
as she watched Joseph
place You
in a stone feeding trough
and heard His first cry?

Did You know, Jesus,
as You felt cold hard stone beneath Your tiny back,
that this infant bed of God-created rock was
a prelude to the stone slab
that would bed Your broken body in final rest?

O Jesus, how majestic is Your name.
The miracles and wonders of Your Advent entrance

will be discovered over and over with marvel
as we ponder, meditate, listen,
enlightenment will not end.

Help us, in this thoroughly secularized era,
return to revel and exuberance,
to true worship at Christmas,
for You showed the way,
went against the norms of Your day.
Your gospel countercultural.

May we who know rebirth
reclaim
for Your sake
sacred honor-driven attention
on the annual adoration of
Your Advent.

AMEN.

Luke 1:32

FORTY

One Day

In this *world* you will have trouble,
You said with authority.
Circumstances difficult,
faith tested to be strengthened
times of tribulation
repeated like rolling waves
before the great and *awesome* Day of the Lord.

Women relate.
Labor pains increase in frequency, intensity, anguish
before a child is born.
So You described our journey home,
wrenching roots from temporal soil
each contraction pushing . . . nearer to eternity,
to transformation
into the Bride of the Lamb.

One day
in the blink of an eye
at the sound of the trumpets

in a moment
at the last call
the gathering will commence in order
and we the perishable will become immortal.

On that day
no longer will there be death;
no mourning
no crying
no pain.
All will be made *new*!

The Lamb will embrace His bride,
her welcome and entrance guaranteed,
our names
written in the Lamb's *book of life*,
and He Himself will wipe away every tear,
soothe and remove every sorrow.

On that day
I will be clean
dressed in white linen
bright, sparkling, radiant
delivered from sin forever,

fears, limitations, weakness
all gone.

In that day,
you will feel no *shame*,
the curse of Eden, gone forever!

On that day
I will see Him face-to-face
will behold His glory
will be with Jesus forever!

I cannot wait!

On that day
I will worship with joy
never grow weary, need rest, or sleep
For there is no night *there*.

Keep me from pessimism, doubt, cynicism,
discouragement, and fear as I wait.
Do not be frightened, You said,
He is *near*, right at the door!
For with You
a *thousand* years is as one day.

May I be ready, watching for Your return,
eager, expectant, alert, ever hopeful
standing near the door,
prepared to fling it open at the first note!

Come quickly, Lord Jesus,
Let the curtain fall.

AMEN.

John 16:33 NIV; Joel 2:31; Revelation 21:4, 27; Zephaniah 3:11 NASB; Revelation 22:5; John 6:20; Matthew 24:33; 2 Peter 3:8

Notes

1. Emily Dickinson, "Tell all the Truth but tell it slant," in *The Complete Works of Emily Dickinson*, ed. Thomas H. Johnson (Boston: Little, Brown and Co., 1960), 506–07.

2. Arthur Bennett, ed., introduction to *The Valley of Vision: A Collection of Puritan Prayers* (1975; repr., Edinburgh and Carlisle, PA: The Banner of Truth Trust, 2019), xix. Page references are to the 2019 edition.

3. Christopher Paolini, *Inheritance* (New York: Alfred A. Knopf, 2011), 343.

4. Laura Story, "Blessings," CD, track 5, *Blessings*, independent, 2011.

5. Thomas Dubay, *The Evidential Power of Beauty: Science and Theology Meet* (San Francisco: Ignatius Press, 1999), 97.

6. Bennett, "Love to Jesus," in *Valley of Vision*, 26.

7. "Christmas Bells," Henry Wadsworth Longfellow, 1863.

8. Longfellow, "Christmas Bells."

9. Dubay, *Evidential Power of Beauty*, 25.

10. Johanna Anderson (lyr.), Dan Forrest (comp.), "Cry No More" (Columbus, OH: Beckenhorst Press, 2011). Used by permission of The Music of Dan Forrest.

11. Dubay, *Evidential Power of Beauty*, 20.

12. "I Surrender All," Judson W. Van DeVenter, 1896.

13. Fleming Rutledge, *Advent: The Once and Future Coming of Jesus Christ* (Grand Rapids, MI: Eerdmans, 2018), 7.

My Heart, Ever His by Barbara Rainey
© 2020 by Ever Thine Home International

Published by Bethany House Publishers
11400 Hampshire Avenue South
Bloomington, Minnesota 55438
www.bethanyhouse.com

Bethany House Publishers is a division of
Baker Publishing Group, Grand Rapids, Michigan

Printed in China

ISBN 978-0-7642-3446-0

Library of Congress Cataloging-in-Publication Control Number: 2019949497

Scripture quotations are from The Holy Bible, English Standard Version® (ESV®), copyright © 2001 by Crossway, a publishing ministry of Good News Publishers. Used by permission. All rights reserved. ESV Text Edition: 2016

Scripture references identified NASB indicate language inspired by the New American Standard Bible® (NASB), copyright © 1960, 1962, 1963, 1968, 1971, 1972, 1973, 1975, 1977, 1995 by The Lockman Foundation. Used by permission. www.Lockman.org

Scripture references identified NIV indicate language inspired by the Holy Bible, New International Version®. NIV®. Copyright © 1973, 1978, 1984, 2011 by Biblica, Inc.™ Used by permission of Zondervan. All rights reserved worldwide. www.zondervan.com. The "NIV" and "New International Version" are trademarks registered in the United States Patent and Trademark Office by Biblica, Inc.™

Cover design by Jennifer Parker
Interior design by William Overbeeke

Author represented by Wolgemuth and Associates

20 21 22 23 24 25 26   7 6 5 4 3 2 1

Barbara Rainey is married to her best friend, Dennis. Their six children are all married, and from these six have come twenty-four grandchildren, who call her Mimi. Her favorite name is to be called "friend" by Jesus. Barbara is increasingly in awe at being chosen and loved by Him.

She is also an artist, author, and ambassador, which tell more about what Barbara loves to do. Together Dennis and Barbara started FamilyLife, a ministry of Cru, in 1976. She speaks at Weekend to Remember marriage conferences and is a frequent guest on *FamilyLife Today*, a nationally syndicated radio program. She coauthored a number of books with her husband and wrote several herself, including *Thanksgiving: A Time to Remember* and *Letters to My Daughters: The Art of Being a Wife*.

Barbara loves to create and make all things beautiful, and one result of that passion is Ever Thine Home, a collection of beautiful and biblical products women can use to make their homes a witness for their faith. Barbara also loves to encourage younger women through her blog. To learn more about Ever Thine Home, read the blogs, subscribe to updates, and more, visit her online at EverThineHome.com.